21 Things Every Future Engineer Should Know

A Practical Guide for Students and Parents

Pat Remick

Frank Cook

KAPLAN) AEC EDUCATION

This publication is designed to provide accurate and authoritative information in regard to the subject matter covered. It is sold with the understanding that the publisher is not engaged in rendering legal, accounting, or other professional service. If legal advice or other expert assistance is required, the services of a competent professional person should be sought.

President: Roy Lipner
Vice-President of Product Development and Publishing: Evan Butterfield
Editorial Project Manager: Laurie McGuire
Director of Production: Daniel Frey
Production Editor: David Shaw
Creative Director: Lucy Jenkins
Typesetter: Janet Schroeder

To Dan and J.D., two extraordinary sons who fill our
lives with laughter and love. Their days of building blocks and
LEGO® creations may be long past, but they remain
the foundation of our lives.

I f books came with truth-in-advertising labels, the warning on this one would be:

"CAUTION: This book is not intended to persuade you to enter the engineering profession; nor is it intended to send you running away as fast as you can. This book is intended to provide a window on a career that many people find incredibly fulfilling, although others find it much less so. We urge you to keep an open mind."

The purpose of this book is really to look at some of the pros and cons of the engineering profession and discuss some of the really good things that can happen for those who make engineering their career choice—without glossing over some of the downsides.

This book is intended for young people who may be wondering whether engineering is the right career for them, as well as the parents, teachers, and counselors who guide them. If you're in high school or the first couple years of college and wondering whether engineering is a profession that suits your skills and interests, this book will help you figure that out, as well as give you a balanced look at the pleasures and challenges of the field. It also suggests some practical steps you can take to prepare yourself for an engineering education and career.

We believe that deciding on a career path is actually more about you than it is about the career—or this book. Over the years we have written a number of "career" books and talked to countless experts in a wide variety of disciplines.

Invariably what career planning comes down to is, "What are you enthusiastic about? What gets you up in the morning and drives you all day? What would you do if you didn't have to worry about making money?"

If the answer is "designing processes and building things that solve problems," then you will find nothing in this book to deter you from an engineering career. If, on the other hand, you'd rather think than do, or theorize rather than build, this book should send up red flags.

As the guidance counselors often say, "Remember: there are no wrong answers here." You can get into a good college with the intent of making a career in engineering and quickly discover that you'd really rather be doing something else. It happens all the time.

In fact, you'd be surprised at the number of people who complete their bachelor's degrees in engineering and then promptly enroll in another course of study for their graduate studies—subjects like law, medicine, or business. An engineering degree establishes an excellent foundation for these other fields.

What's great about engineering is that, at its most rudimentary level, it is a way of "looking at things." At a poetry reading, are you more interested in the poetry or the mechanics of the microphone system? When a jet flies overhead, are you more interested in where it's going or how it stays aloft? When you walk into a house, do you care about the décor or do you wonder how many walls you could remove and still leave it standing?

As you read through this book, one of the things you'll note is that there are no equations here. Aside from some occasional statistics, the only numbers you'll find in this book are the page numbers.

This is very much a layperson's book.

Make no mistake, however: If you are intent on becoming an engineer, you have to do the math. An interest in—and enjoyment of—math and physical sciences are as essential to the engineer as a hammer is to a carpenter.

Do you have to be a bit of a nerd to be an engineer? Consider this assessment from National Academy of Engineering President William A. Wulf in an address to a workshop on diversity in engineering:

"If engineers were as dull as they are in the popular stereotype, they wouldn't be good engineers. They wouldn't have the life experiences they need to come up with creative solutions to human problems. Let me repeat. If engineers were really as dull as the stereotype, they wouldn't be good engineers!"

Still . . .

- If you've ever looked at a TV remote control and wondered what it would take to turn it into a ray gun, you could be an engineer at heart.
- If you think the comic strip "Dilbert" is a documentary, then this could be the profession for you.
- If you have a pet named after a scientist . . . well, let's not dwell on it.

Finally, please think of this as a workbook. If there is something you find important, feel free to take a pen and underline it. If you want to come back to a section later, feel free to dog-ear the page. If your weapon of choice is a highlighter, go crazy.

Make this book work for you. Your inner engineer approves!

I n the course of our research for this book, we had conversations with academics, many heads of professional societies, countless working engineers, and others.

A short list of those to whom we are grateful, beyond all of the wonderful sources we have quoted in the book, includes:

Kathy Tollerton, the extremely helpful public affairs manager for the American Society for Engineering Education, and its director of data research, Michael Gibbons; Stacey Ober and her staff at the National Society of Professional Engineers; the folks at the Bureau of Labor Statistics, including Howard Haghye; and John Varrasi of the American Society of Mechanical Engineers.

Several reviewers read the manuscript for this book and provided very helpful insight and recommendations. The publisher and authors are grateful to:

Douglas R. Carroll, PhD, University of Missouri, Rolla
Candace Christy Hickey, PE, Hunt Engineering Company
Susan L. Murray, PhD, PE, University of Missouri, Rolla

Finally, we'd like to thank the numerous professionals at Kaplan Professional Publishing for their faith in this project and their tireless efforts to see it through to the end.

Pat Remick and Frank Cook

CHAPTER 1

Engineering: Turning Ideas into Realities

Membership in this prestigious society is still open

"Scientists study the world as it is, engineers create the world that never has been."
— *Theodore Von Karman, engineer, rocket scientist*

Imagine yourself being part of it—that long line of innovators that stretches back to the beginning of time, that string of individuals who brought civilization forward step-by-step by looking at some human task and bragging:

"I can make something that does that," or "I can build something that does that *better*."

Imagine being a member of the prestigious group that built both the pyramids and the space shuttle, and that constructed the aqueducts that allowed water to flow to Rome and the canal that allowed water to flow across Panama.

Imagine being part of the connection that runs from the first man who figured out that a saddle could stabilize a rider on the back of a horse to the automotive engineers of today who figured out that seatbelts and airbags could save lives.

Now imagine being stuck in front of a computer for endless hours in the bowels of some giant corporation or completing a building that is awarded a prize but it's the architect whose picture is on the cover of *Newsweek*.

Welcome to the pros and cons of the engineering profession.

If you decide that the pros outweigh the cons, the good news is that membership in this society is still open and you are more than welcome to join it.

The story of engineering is nothing less than the story of human ingenuity. It is that infinitely long list of inventions and accomplishments—from the first plow to the modern computer—that touch our everyday lives. Nevertheless, it also is the story of men and women often overlooked for praise, sometimes dismissed as social misfits, and who must spend a lifetime trying to keep up with the very innovations that are driving their own profession.

In the preparation of this book, we went to a host of those engineers—those just starting out, as well as those who have reached the top of their careers—and asked them basically what they would tell a group of parents and students if they were sitting in a casual setting discussing the field of engineering.

We asked them to talk about how a parent could identify a budding engineer early in a child's life and how that interest could be encouraged. We even talked about whether such an interest should be encouraged at all, or whether parents should just allow "nature to take its course."

We talked at length about the practical aspects of eventually getting a job as an engineer and what kind of educational background a student must have to even be considered by major engineering schools. We discussed salaries and found some numbers we think will interest you—and a few that will disappoint.

In our conversations, we even went so far as to discuss why so many people leave the engineering profession every year. Are they simply finding better opportunities elsewhere or is something driving them out?

This book is a summary of those conversations—literally, a report on the positives and negatives of the industry that we've distilled down to 21 ideas ranging from the very practical to the largely philosophical. All are intended to provide those on the outside—who may be thinking about coming in—with a glimpse of what the profession looks like on the inside.

The 21 Things

So, what are the "21 Things" you might wonder about engineering? Basically, they sound a little like this:

1. "If I put together blocks as a baby and built towering structures with LEGOs, am I an engineer at heart?" Maybe, but more realistically those are things all children like to do at early ages. The most common trait in young people who go on to be engineers is genuine curiosity—plus some affection for math and science. (Chapter 2)
2. "How wide of a profession is engineering?" Finding an element of society that is untouched by engineers is just about impossible. Engineers are working everywhere from the icecaps to the Sahara Desert, from the bottom of the ocean to outer space. Somewhere in there you're going to find something you like. (Chapter 3)
3. "What if I'm female?" The days of engineering being solely a men's club are beginning to decline, but the only way to make sure they are gone forever is for you to prove it to yourself. Engineering offers a "boundless universe" for women. Come explore it. (Chapter 4)
4. "What if I'm Black, Hispanic, or Native American?" There's plenty of room in engineering for everyone and lots of groups to support you—as long as you can get the academic preparation every engineering student needs, regardless of race or sex. (Chapter 5)
5. "What do I need to do in high school?" We can't say it enough—you need to take lots of math and science and be fairly competent in both subjects. Outside of the classroom, there's a huge variety of stimulating and fun activities available to expose you to some of the many fascinating facets of engineering. (Chapter 6)
6. "How do I pick a college? Or get a college to pick me?" Investing some time in thinking about the type of engineering you want to study does make it a little easier to figure out where to go. But if you have no idea which engineering discipline is for you, don't be overly concerned. You're not

alone and you have options, although it will be important to find a program with the ABET seal of approval. (Chapter 7)

7. "Why do students leave?" For a variety of reasons, some engineering students never become working engineers. With some guidance, hard work, and a bit of fun, you won't be one of them. (Chapter 8)

8. "Is there anywhere I can go to get help before, during, and/or after college?" Is there ever! The number of institutions, societies, and academies in the engineering profession seems to be boundless, every one dedicated to keeping you up-to-date. (Chapter 9)

9. "If I become an engineer, can I get a job?" You bet. Engineering skills tend to be in need regardless of the economy. In addition, your college and the professional societies have resources to help in your job search. (Chapters 10 and 11)

10. "How do I get started?" You can start your career with a large or small company, profit or nonprofit enterprise, government organization or public firm. You can even start your own business, though that can be tough. (Chapter 12)

11. "What about the global economy?" Not all engineers or engineering jobs are in the United States. You should understand the challenges—and opportunities—this implies. (Chapter 13)

12. "Do I have to have a license?" Not always, but... It would be a good idea to get one even if you aren't required to have one. Licensing is required for those who may be involved in projects with concerns for public safety, such as civil engineers, and it's also a good idea if someday you hope to do expert witnessing or consulting. Licensing also is seen as evidence of high professional standards, resulting in higher compensation. (Chapter 14)

13. "Will I ever be allowed to do what I want to do?" The good news is "yes," entrepreneurs have a big place in this industry although in all honesty, funding is sometimes hard to come by. (Chapter 15)

14. "Can't the computer do everything an engineer can do?" There is no doubt that the profession is changing and computers are doing more of the math. But you still need

someone to tell a computer what to do, someone to tell the computer how to do it, and someone who knows whether the computer is doing it right. (Chapter 16)

15. "I don't really need a head for business, right?" Wrong. Engineers increasingly must understand the economics of their projects with respect to the larger organization. They also must understand business politics, culture, and organization in order to sell their ideas to managers, clients, and other stakeholders. (Chapter 17)

16. "Do I have to speak a language other than mathematics?" Yes, and competently. Engineers have a reputation when it comes to writing and communicating with others, and it's not a good one. (Chapter 18)

17. "I'd really rather be left alone to work on my project." Wouldn't we all? In the old days you could sit at your desk and calculate all day, but today you need to work and play well with others. More employers want teams, not lone wolves. (Also in Chapter 18)

18. "Should I call my lawyer?" You probably should if you've invented anything. Engineers create things and lawyers help them protect their intellectual property. Contract compliance and product liability are other issues that bring engineers and lawyers together. (Chapter 19)

19. "Am I going to be held to any standard?" Ethics have become such an issue in the engineering world that many colleges have added ethics classes to their engineering curriculum. Just because you can figure out a way to build it doesn't mean that you should. (Chapter 20)

20. "What if I get into engineering and don't like it?" The disciplines and processes learned in engineering apply in almost all walks of life. Engineers don't just develop products and build systems. You can find them in economics and marketing, as CEOs of Fortune 500 companies, and even presidents of the United States. (Chapter 21)

21. "What does the future hold?" Everything imaginable: biomedicine, robotics, aerospace, computers, nanotechnology. Everywhere you look, there you are. (Chapter 22)

The Engineering "Crisis"

In our research for the 21 things every future engineer should know, we discovered an ongoing discussion of whether there is a "crisis" in the engineering profession. The answer, we've concluded, is a resounding "yes," and then again, "no."

At the core of the issue is whether America's future will be innovated, developed, and built by homegrown Americans, or by people born in other countries who sell their skills to the United States, conceivably at ever higher prices. The question is whether enough engineers are coming out of American schools to meet America's current and future demands.

Make no mistake: the demand will be met regardless of where the engineers come from. As engineers themselves will tell you, one of the first laws of physics is that, in one way or another, vacuums will be filled.

In some ways it's already happening.

Today in America, somewhere between 2 million and 3 million people call themselves engineers. Every year some of these engineers leave their jobs to retire or pursue other lines of work. In addition, the number of U.S. jobs requiring science and engineering training is expected to grow for the foreseeable future. Some observers say that not enough new engineers are graduating from U.S. schools to fill the positions that will open up over time. Partly in response to this opportunity gap, a large number of foreign nationals with foreign engineering degrees have entered the United States to work.

Still, it also needs to be noted that what the United States calls an engineer and what other countries call an engineer tend to be different things. Many states and individual disciplines have exacting academic standards that must be met before someone can call themselves an "engineer." In other parts of the world, skills sets and academic requirements may not be nearly so demanding.

Working against this influx from abroad is the fact that immigration and security concerns are making it more difficult for the foreign-born to enter the United States legally. In addition, other parts of the developing world are creating global competition for their talent.

And although the question of the "engineering crisis" came up in almost every conversation we had with engineers, teachers, administrators, and researchers, the surprising thing was that there were no consistent answers on how to solve it.

Clearly the opportunities (let's be blunt: the jobs and the money) will be out there for those who have the skills to enter the profession. The question is whether you have the calling and the discipline to push yourself forward.

We will tell you this: Of the many engineers we talked to, not one regretted his or her choice of profession.

Now that you've had an overview of what every future engineer should know, the next step is determining whether you're also an engineer at heart.

CHAPTER 2

You Might Be a Future Engineer

And you don't have to be a super-brilliant white guy either

No engineer looks at a television remote
control without wondering what it
would take to turn it into a stun gun.

—Industry cliché

Here are a couple of wonderful facts to keep in mind as you read this chapter:

1. There aren't enough engineers to fill all of the engineering jobs in the United States.
2. New college graduates with engineering degrees make significantly more money than other college graduates.

Engineering sounds like a pretty good profession to choose, doesn't it?

Now, let's make sure you know that we're not talking about the folks who are in charge of trains, or the maintenance men who wear "building engineer" patches on their uniforms. Nor are we discussing the job title that some homemakers prefer—that of "domestic" engineer. Furthermore, you may be surprised to know that we're also not talking about the men and women who do computer programming and call themselves "software engineers" (more about that in Chapter 3).

We're talking about men and women who are specifically trained in how to use math and science to solve practical problems. Most of them pursue at least a four-year college degree in some branch of engineering.

"Where does science become engineering? Science is everything—naturally. Once you turn it into a soda can, by applying math and science, it becomes engineering," says Leann Yoder, executive director of the Junior Engineering Technology Society (JETS).

Right now you may be thinking: Don't I have to be a super-smart white guy with pasty skin, thick glasses, and a pocket protector to be an engineer?

Are you really asking: Do I have to be a nerd?

The answers are: No, and definitely not.

More Creativity than Brilliance

"The engineering profession certainly has what you might say is a perception about it by high school students that you have to be absolutely brilliant in math and science to be a successful engineer," says Dr. David A. Wormley, president-elect of the American Society for Engineering Education.

"One of the things people neglect to talk about is that engineering is a very creative profession and that people can be successful with a variety of backgrounds and goals," says Wormley, also dean of engineering at Penn State. "The fact that engineering is extremely creative isn't emphasized very much."

To try to rectify the problem, Wormley says, his engineering college has joined with Penn State's college of education to develop a course for teachers on how to introduce the creative aspects of engineering into grade school and high school classrooms so students will understand how much of engineering involves creative problem-solving.

There are even those who believe that being too brilliant in math and science can be a handicap in the engineering world.

"I think it has to be somebody who has a good aptitude for math [and] science. I don't think you necessarily have to be brilliant. I'm not so sure the brilliant ones make the best engineers," says Steve Parkinson, a licensed civil engineer who heads up the

Public Works Department in Portsmouth, New Hampshire. "They tend to be on a higher plane: they can't relate to other people. They're more research people. They tend to be theorists. You need to be able to relate to people, especially in civil engineering. Not only do you need math and science, you also need communication skills."

Still, math and science are the gateways.

Says Douglas R. Carroll at the University of Missouri, Rolla, one of the top engineering schools in the country, "I've worked with freshmen students for the last 15 years as a freshman advisor, helping them get through the calculus, chemistry, and physics, and experiencing how difficult it is for some students. The main problem is calculus: most of the students who give up usually give up because they cannot pass calculus. Students who took the advanced math track in high school and made a lot of Cs will have a difficult time getting through the math courses at a top engineering college."

The Parent Factor

So while you do need to be competent in math and science, brilliance is optional. Your gender and ethnic background don't matter either. There is room in engineering for all kinds of people—maybe your parents already think you belong there.

It could be they've already seen some promising signs of what they want to believe is your natural engineering aptitude: You built huge towers from baby blocks or created intricate structures and cities with LEGOs®. Perhaps you've been a math whiz since everyone can remember.

Maybe you're the type of person who likes to take things apart to see how they work and then try to put them back together so they work better. Your parents might have hated seeing the television remote control or computer in pieces, but their heart skipped a beat when they saw you could reconstruct them. Sure, they might have sometimes found it annoying that you had to know the "why's" and "how's" about everything, but it also might have given them a dream for your future.

Yes, these can all be indications that engineering might be a good career path for you to consider—or maybe not.

The Student Most Likely to . . .

If there is one primary truth about engineering it is that you have to like math and science. You don't have to be gifted in these subjects, but you do have to like and be competent in them because you're going to spend a lot of time using them. You also should rank in at least the top half of your high school class.

Moreover, you really have to like solving problems. Because that's what engineers do: they use logic and science to solve problems. They invent, they build, and they make things better.

As you'll see in the next chapter, there are many types of engineers. Some need more math skills than others. There are those engineers who are totally hands-on and others who are great thinkers who work in labs all day. However, every engineering discipline requires three important attributes—creativity, persistence, and a desire to improve things.

Do you think you have what it takes to become an engineer?

This is not a question to be answered lightly. Consider that as many as half of the students who enter college to study engineering leave the discipline, often doing so even before they choose their specific course of engineering study, according to the American Society for Engineering Education. Other estimates put the number as high as 60 percent. That should be reason enough to give careful thought about the field of engineering.

This high attrition rate is an area of very great concern to the industry and among educators. They agree that they need to do a far better job of helping students figure out if engineering is right for them. There are lots of engineering groups out there that are trying to find ways to help potential engineers discover whether engineering could be a good fit. Many are involved in trying to get engineering into more grade school and high school classrooms, but to date Massachusetts is the only state that includes engineering skills in its curriculum standards.

Some of the groups have developed self-tests with questions that can help you try to figure out whether you belong in engineering. Here are a few sample questions to consider:

- Are you curious about things?
- Do you like to solve problems?
- Do you understand basic math fundamentals?
- Does math come easy to you or do you struggle to get the concepts?
- Do you enjoy knowing how things work?
- Do you like mazes and jigsaw puzzles?
- Can you recognize patterns, shapes, or objects and how they relate to an overall picture?
- Do you like computers, video games, and technology in general?
- Can you speak and write clearly?
- Do you have abstract reasoning skills? In other words, can you take theoretical information, inferences, and/or implications to analyze things and then make decisions?
- Do you work well with others?
- Do you like to think up new ways to do things?

"Yes" answers indicate you have qualities that are important in engineering. If you answered "no" to most of the questions, engineering might not be the career path for you.

You also need to know that there are certain prerequisites to beginning an engineering course of study in college: lots of high school math, math, and more math and oh yeah, science, too.

If you're in high school now and don't have this preparation, don't despair. There are ways to get around this problem. We'll talk more about preparation in Chapter 6 but for now, just figure that it might mean taking some extra courses over the summer, or spending a semester or two at a community college. You might even consider getting an engineering technology associate's two-year degree first. See Chapter 6 for more about this option.

Remember: engineering is all about solving problems. If you won't have the math and science courses you need to enter a college engineering program, that's the first problem you're going to need to solve.

And once you get into college, well, it's not going to be the easiest course of study to follow but hard work and persistence are what make engineers. There will be lots of people available to help you along the way, from your professors to mentors in the community, to professional societies. All of them want to see you succeed.

Time to Explore

But first you should learn a little more about engineering. This book will help you with that.

There also are many Internet resources with a multitude of information aimed at various age levels to promote the engineering field. Some of them have a variety of tools to help you hone in on whether you have the characteristics of an engineer.

Granted, these resources are all extremely positive about the field. You'll need to read the rest of this book to learn more about the nitty-gritty they might not tell you about. Nonetheless, it won't hurt to do a little online exploring of the engineering field in general:

- JETS, the Junior Engineering Technical Society, is a non-profit education organization established in 1950, "to inform and excite young people about careers in engineering." It serves over 30,000 students through its various programs. These include the National Engineering Aptitude Search+ (NEAS+), an academic self-assessment that helps high school students determine their strengths and weaknesses in subject areas critical to engineering and technology. It also provides information on various engineering careers via mail and at *www.jets.org*.
- Try an online test to determine "what kind of smart are you?" Sponsored by the National Action Council for Minorities in Engineering, the "Guide Me" Web site has several resources to help young people from all backgrounds figure

out whether engineering is right for them. It's at *www.guide-menacme.org.*

- The American Society for Engineering Education has put together a Web site at *www.engineeringk12.org* that explores a variety of disciplines and includes self-assessment options.
- National Engineers Week has a Web site with an assortment of information about the profession called *www.discoverengineering.org.*
- "Is Engineering for You?" Whether you're male or female, you might want to check out the K-12 Programs section at *www.swe.org* to find information about engineering developed by the Society of Women Engineers.

Here are some non-Internet ways to explore whether engineering might be a good match for you:

- **Participate in fun engineering-related activities**—Numerous programs and competitions exist that are aimed at introducing young people to the various dimensions of engineering. We'll talk about them more in Chapter 6 but a few examples are FIRST Robotics, Math Counts, and the American Computer Science League.
- **Job shadowing**—Spend some time with real engineers to see what they do and how they spend their workdays. Take part of a day, an entire day, or a couple of days. This can help give you a revealing look at the real world of engineering.
- **Summer jobs and internships**—If you're interested in engineering, you might consider trying to get a job in an engineering office. Maybe as a high school student you'll just be filing paperwork or answering the phone, but it will give you an unparalleled bird's eye view of the day-to-day lives of the engineers working there. At the college level, internships are an even better option.
- **Summer camps**—Various organizations offer math and science camps, including some programs that are specific to engineering. Local universities often host them as part of their K-12 outreach programs.

Now, let's take a look at the kinds of engineering that are out there so you'll have a better idea of why this could be the career choice for you.

CHAPTER 3

Engineering Disciplines

What kind of engineer should you be?

"Mechanical engineers make weapons, civil engineers make targets."
*   –Classic engineering joke*

E ngineers touch every part of our lives, from the moment we get up in the morning until we go to bed at night. They can be found at the bottom of the ocean, in space, and so many places in between all around the world, from deserts to polar icecaps to next door.

Their inventions and products are everywhere. They keep the heat and air-conditioning on, the water flowing, food growing, buildings standing, our vehicles on the road, our planes in the sky, our spacecraft in the heavens, and our ships on the sea. They make our toys, the things we need to live, and the tools we use for work. They will develop products and processes to make our lives better now and in the future. They will continue to bring things into our world that we don't even realize we need.

So, how wide is this profession? It's as far as your imagination can take you. If you were to count up all of the jobs that need an "engineer" to fill them, you would have a nearly endless list of possibilities.

Things may become a little less clear, however, when you try to figure out which one is right for you.

What you need to know is this: The U.S. government keeps statistics on 17 separate engineering disciplines. Keep in mind, though, that each of these major disciplines may have numerous specialty areas with an incredible amount of variety. Some of them are so well-known that it might seem surprising that they haven't warranted their own "discipline" status in the eyes of government statisticians.

For most of the world, it really doesn't matter how many types of engineers exist. But when you are considering engineering as a possible career path, you need to know the main routes to get there. Otherwise, how will you even know which course of study to follow to obtain that four- or five-year college degree that is the highway to engineering?

So let's try to take a look at some of the options. We've provided you with an alphabetized list of what most would agree are the primary engineering disciplines. Each has courses of study accredited by ABET, the recognized Accreditation Board for Engineering and Technology programs in colleges and universities.

As you review these listings, think about the things that interest you. Take advantage of opportunities to think like a true engineer—"outside the box." As you read about each category, take note of some of the specialty areas within it. You may be surprised to find something that interests you in a discipline you'd least expect. It is also not uncommon for an engineer trained in one discipline to work in another related branch, such as a mechanical engineer working in chemical engineering.

In addition, keep in mind that some of the "endless possibilities" awaiting you in engineering may not even exist until you create them. That's what engineering is all about.

Do You Love Things That Fly?

Aerospace engineers design, develop, and test aircraft and spacecraft ranging from rockets and spacecraft to gliders and small passenger aircraft, and everything in between. If they deal only with aircraft, they sometimes are known as **aeronautical** engineers, while those who work just with spacecraft may be called **astronautical** engineers.

Aerospace engineers develop new technologies for aviation, space exploration, and defense systems. Some specialize in a particular type of plane, missile, or spacecraft. Others may concentrate on areas of manufacturing, design, or navigation systems, or they might investigate aviation accidents and system failures.

- **Cool things you could do**—Build things to explore or colonize space; make military airplanes go faster; develop more efficient commercial airliners; or investigate crashes.
- **Specialty areas include**—Commercial or military aerospace; engineering, science, and data processing; and inspection and compliance officers.
- **Education**—Aerospace engineers must have at least a four-year college degree. Some schools consider this field to be a division of mechanical engineering, but most aeronautical engineers have degrees in aeronautic or aerospace engineering. There are about 60 ABET-accredited aerospace programs. Some aerospace engineers also have advanced degrees in physics, aerodynamics, or astronautics. A master's degree is recommended to have an effective career in the research and development industry.
- **Working**—Although many aeronautical engineers work for such U.S. government agencies as NASA and the Defense Department, far more work for government contractors in the aircraft manufacturing and/or repair, space, or guided missile industries. Some are employed in commercial aviation, and several teach or work in research labs.
- **Average starting salaries in 2005**—Bachelor's—$50,993, master's—$62,930, and PhD—$72,529.
- **Employment outlook**—In 2005, there were 81,100 employed aerospace engineers earning a median annual income of $85,450. Aerospace engineers constituted about 5 percent of the total number of engineers employed in the 17 major fields. New jobs are likely to be generated in the aerospace area, but the commercial aircraft sector is expected to decline due to increased efficiency. Overall, this field is expected to grow by no more than 8 percent through 2014, but the outlook is still favorable because a previous per-

ceived lack of opportunities in the field led to fewer granted degrees and new graduates are needed to replace engineers leaving the field.

- **Industries with highest levels of employment and annual mean wage (May 2005)**

Industry	Employment level	Annual mean wage
Aerospace product and parts manufacturing	40,860	$80,920
Electronic instrument manufacturing	13,040	$90,630
Federal government	7,680	$93,050
Architectural and engineering services	7,410	$89,400
Scientific research and development services	4,740	$94,780

- **Top-paying states with number employed and annual mean wage**

State	Employment level	Annual mean wage
Nevada	Unavailable	$126,820
Virginia	4,210	$100,490
California	24,260	$93,050
New Mexico	180	$91,740
Massachusetts	970	$90,650

- **Most current numbers**—*www.bls.gov/oes/current/oes172011.htm*
- **More information**—American Institute of Aeronautics and Astronautics, *www.aiaa.org*

Do You Want to Feed People While Conserving the Environment?

Agricultural engineers are involved in every aspect of our food supply.

They create new technology for agricultural, food, and biological systems. This includes irrigation systems, farming equipment and structures, and food processing.

Agricultural engineers research and devise ways to: conserve water use and prevent erosion; make sure the proper nutrients reach crops; improve crop and livestock production; extend the storage life of perishable products like fruits and vegetables or flowers; deal with agricultural waste, and design machinery.

- **Cool things you could do**—Figure out how to grow crops in small spaces; expand fish-farming; find a way to control insects with fewer pesticides; or improve food safety.
- **Specialty areas include**—Power systems and machinery design; structures and environment engineering; and food and bioprocess engineering.
- **Education**—The majority of agricultural engineering jobs require a four-year college degree. There are 40 ABET-accredited agricultural engineering programs, but some agricultural engineers obtain their degrees in mechanical, civil, chemical, or electrical engineering.
- **Working**—Agricultural engineers work in a variety of areas, including research and development, production, sales, and management. The federal or state governments employ more than one-fifth of agricultural engineers. They also might work directly with farmers, agribusiness, or conservation groups.
- **Average starting salaries in 2005**—Bachelor's—$46,172 and master's—$53,022.
- **Employment outlook**—In 2005, there were 3,170 employed agricultural engineers earning a mean annual income of $66,370. This is the smallest of the 17 major specialties. However, expect a 9- to 17-percent growth in employment opportunities through the year 2014, primarily due to the

growing interest in worldwide standardization of agricultural equipment. As the population increases, expect more of a need for these engineers to develop more efficient agricultural production while conserving resources.

- **Industries with highest levels of employment and annual mean wage (May 2005)**

Industry	Employment level	Annual mean wage
Architectural and engineering services	550	$71,640
Federal government	390	$68,070
Colleges and universities	170	$53,660
Misc. nondurable goods merchant wholesalers	150	$74,270
Animal slaughtering and processing	140	$61,300

- **Top-paying states with number employed and annual mean wage**

State	Employment level	Annual mean wage
North Carolina	50	$83,370
Maryland	Unavailable	$77,230
New York	Unavailable	$75,220
Illinois	Unavailable	$72,540
Missouri	90	$72,540

- **Most current numbers—***www.bls.gov/oes/current/oes172021.htm*
- **More information—**American Society of Agricultural and Biological Engineers, *www.asabe.org*

Enjoy Biology and Interested in Medicine?

Biomedical engineers use technology to research and develop procedures and devices to treat or alleviate medical and health-related problems.

They invent medicines or better manufacturing processes to make them; create artificial devices to substitute for worn, injured, or missing body parts (such as hearing aids, cardiac pacemakers, and artificial joints); and find ways to use electronics or mechanics to help people.

They also deal with information systems, medical instruments, and physical therapy devices. Biomedical engineers also are more involved with safety, regulatory, and biological issues than other types of engineers.

- **Cool things you could do**—Prevent sports injuries; help paralyzed people walk; build bionic arms and legs; or find ways to manufacture new AIDS and cancer medicines.
- **Specialty areas include**—Biomaterials, biomechanics, medical imaging, rehabilitation engineering, and orthopedic engineering.
- **Education**—A minimum of a four-year college degree is required. Knowledge of human anatomy and physiology is important. A few programs use **"biomedical engineering"** synonymously with **bioengineering.** There are 36 ABET-accredited bioengineering bachelor's degree programs, but most biomedical engineers also have a background in another engineering discipline, such as mechanical engineering or electronics. A graduate degree is necessary for many entry-level jobs. About one-third of those receiving four-year biomedical degrees continue on to medical school.
- **Working**—Many biomedical engineers work in research laboratories.
- **Average starting salaries in 2005**—Bachelor's—$48,503 and master's—$59,667.
- **Employment outlook**—In 2005, there were 11,660 employed biomedical engineers earning a mean annual salary of $75,380. Although this currently is among the smaller engi-

neering fields, interest in the field is increasing along with an aging population. In addition, a growing demand for more sophisticated medical devices and procedures will require more biomedical engineers. Employment is expected to grow by 27 percent or more by 2014.

- **Industries with highest levels of employment and annual mean wage (May 2005)**

Industry	Employment level	Annual mean wage
Scientific research and development services	2,450	$86,960
Medical equipment and supplies manufacturing	2,160	$74,780
Pharmaceutical and medicine manufacturing	2,000	$76,510
General medical and surgical hospitals	1,470	$55,510
Electronic instrument manufacturing	1,150	$72,260

- **Top-paying states with number employed and annual mean wage**

State	Employment level	Annual mean wage
Virginia	90	$92,290
Massachusetts	1,330	$86,010
California	2,410	$84,450
Maryland	380	$84,330
New York	Unavailable	$82,340

- **Most current numbers**—*www.bls.gov/oes/current/oes172031.htm*
- **More information**—Biomedical Engineering Network, *www.bmenet.org*

Enjoy Chemistry and the Challenge of Finding New Approaches?

Chemical engineers use chemistry to transform raw materials into useful products and they also solve problems related to chemical production and use. They may figure out how to control pollution and treat waste, develop hardier strains of food, map the human genome, purify water or develop medicines.

Chemical engineers work in such areas as petrochemicals, refining, specialty chemicals, biotechnologies, nanotechnologies, electronics, and information technologies. Engineers involved in the design and maintenance of chemical processes for large-scale manufacturing may be called "process engineers."

- **Cool things you could do—**Invent a new kind of toothpaste; find a new way to make ice cream; create cleaner and better fuel sources; or help crops resist disease.
- **Specialty areas include—**Biochemical, food, process, pharmaceutical, environmental control, and safety engineering.
- **Education—**A four-year college degree is needed. Generally, chemical engineers must be familiar with both chemistry and mechanical engineering. There are 156 ABET-accredited chemical engineering programs, but some have specialized degrees in biochemical, petroleum, metallurgical, or sanitation engineering. About 20 percent of chemical engineers go on to graduate school, or pursue other careers such as medicine or becoming patent attorneys.
- **Working—**About one-fourth of chemical engineers are in the chemical industry but another 20 percent work in other manufacturing industries, such as paper and pulp, semiconductors, clothing, and pharmaceuticals. They may work in research and development labs, production plants, or management. Some provide engineering services as consultants and others teach.
- **Average starting salaries in 2005—**Bachelor's—$53,813, master's—$57,260, and PhD—$79,591.
- **Employment outlook—**In 2005, there were 27,550 engineers earning a mean annual income of $79,230. Expect an average

job growth of 9 to 17 percent in this field through 2014, although an overall employment decline is expected in the chemical manufacturing industry. Pharmaceuticals may provide the best manufacturing employment opportunities. Job growth also is expected in scientific research and development, especially in biotechnology, nanotechnology, and energy.

- **Industries with highest levels of employment and annual mean wage (May 2005)**

Industry	Employment level	Annual mean wage
Architectural and engineering services	4,160	$80,430
Basic chemical manufacturing	3,760	$78,900
Scientific research and development services	2,930	$88,670
Resin, rubber, and artificial fibers manufacturing	1,870	$78,820
Petroleum and coal products manufacturing	1,590	$83,440

- **Top-paying states with number employed and annual mean wage**

State	Employment level	Annual mean wage
Idaho	180	$95,470
District of Columbia	110	$90,120
Louisiana	1,110	$87,870
Virginia	1,120	$86,650
Alaska	30	$86,370

- **Most current numbers**—*www.bls.gov/oes/current/oes172041.htm*
- **More information**—American Institute of Chemical Engineers, *www.aiche.org*

Like to Build Things?

Civil engineers plan, design, and supervise the building and maintenance of different kinds of structures—including buildings, bridges, dams, roads, tunnels, and airports. They may also deal with flood control, traffic, and water supply and sewage systems. From the pyramids to today, this engineering discipline is one of the oldest and broadest, with numerous specialties. It also is the largest engineering field.

Civil engineers often must take into account construction costs, potential environmental hazards, government regulations, safety, and a project's expected lifespan. Many civil engineers hold administrative or supervisory positions, such as city engineer or construction project supervisor.

Note: Any engineer who provides engineering services to the public or represents him- or herself as a civil engineer must be licensed in the state where he or she is practicing. (See Chapter 14.)

- **Cool things you could do**—Build skyscrapers, tunnels, or bridges; design amusement rides; create the airports of the future; or make things safe from tornadoes and hurricanes.
- **Specialty areas include**—Architectural, structural, construction, environmental, geotechnical, hydraulic/hydrology/water, material science, transportation, and surveying.
- **Education**—A four-year college degree is required for most civil engineering jobs, and a master's degree is being recommended by some for licensure and practice. Many civil engineers seek engineering bachelor's degrees specific to their preferred specialty area, such as water resources or structural engineering. There are 193 ABET-accredited civil engineering programs.
- **Licensure requirements**—These vary by state, but all states require two licensure exams to be passed: Fundamentals of Engineering exam and the Principles and Practice exam (called the PE), plus completion of a state-mandated number of years of work under a licensed Professional Engineer's supervision. Some states allow a person to substitute additional years of supervised work experience for a college

degree, but all accept a four-year Bachelor of Science (BS) or Bachelor of Engineering (BEng) in Civil Engineering. There also are international engineering agreements allowing engineers to practice across borders.

■ **Working**—Civil engineers are wherever people build things. They may work out of offices or in labs, but most are at construction sites.

■ **Average starting salaries in 2005**—Bachelor's—$43,679, master's—$48,050, and PhD—$59,625.

■ **Employment outlook**—There are more civil engineering jobs than college programs can provide graduates to fill. In 2005, there were 229,700 employed civil engineers earning a mean annual income of $69,480. Expect an average employment growth of 9 to 17 percent through 2014, due to general population growth requiring higher capacity transportation, water supply, and pollution control systems. There also will be the expected need to replace or repair existing structures. Opportunities for those involved in construction and related industries will vary by geographic area and economic conditions.

■ **Industries with highest levels of employment and annual mean wage (May 2005)**

Industry	Employment level	Annual mean wage
Architectural and engineering services	115,810	$71,010
State government	31,280	$62,100
Local government	28,960	$69,240
Nonresidential building construction	10,640	$65,940
Federal government	8,800	$77,230

- **Top-paying states with number employed and annual mean wage**

State	Employment level	Annual mean wage
District of Columbia	870	$83,010
California	38,530	$76,070
Nevada	2,620	$76,000
New Jersey	6,220	$75,560
Nebraska	1,420	$75,000

- **Most current numbers**—*www.bls.gov/oes/current/oes172051.htm*
- **More information**—American Society of Civil Engineers, *www.asce.org*

Are Computers Your Thing?

Computer hardware engineers research, design, develop, test, and oversee the installation of the computer systems that keep things going in our lives, from our cars and traffic lights to our toaster ovens and heart pacemakers—plus so much in between.

While their work is similar to what electronics engineers do, computer engineers work exclusively with computers, computer systems, and computer-related equipment such as chips, circuit boards, keyboards, modems, and printers. Computer engineers also analyze system requirements, design networks, and work on a system's software.

- **Cool things you could do**—Build a computer system for a vehicle to explore the planets or our roads; make a hot new product work; or build something to do your chores.
- **Specialty areas include**—Computer architecture, design, and quality control.
- **Education**—Most computer hardware engineers have bachelor's degrees in computer engineering or electrical engi-

neering. There are 174 ABET-accredited bachelor's degree programs specific to computer engineering.

- **Working—**More than 40 percent of computer hardware engineers work in computer and electronic product manufacturing. Computer engineers can work anywhere there are computers, and telecommuting is common. They often work with teams of scientists or engineers from other disciplines.
- **Average computer hardware starting salaries in 2005—** Bachelor's—$52,464, master's—$60,354, and PhD—$69,625.

Software Engineering

There is controversy over whether software "engineering" is a separate discipline from computer engineering or even engineering at all. Some believe more appropriate terms are "software development" or "computer programming," and note that an engineering degree is not necessary for these jobs.

In addition, there are no widely accepted criteria for distinguishing software engineers and the industry is in a debate on their licensing. The U.S. government does not include software engineering as one of the 17 engineering disciplines it tracks.

- **Employment outlook—**In 2005, there were 78,580 computer hardware engineers making an annual mean income of $87,170. Computer hardware engineers constitute just over 5 percent of the engineering workforce, and job growth through 2014 is expected to be average, ranging from 9 to 17 percent. This may seem surprising, giving the rapid expansion in the use of information technology. However, intense foreign competition is expected to restrict U.S. job growth in this field. Much of the U.S. expansion is anticipated to be in computer system design and related services because computer and semiconductor manufacturers are contracting out an increasing amount of their engineering needs.

■ **Industries with highest levels of employment and annual mean wage (May 2005)**

Industry	Employment level	Annual mean wage
Semiconductor and electronic component manufacturing	14,440	$89,870
Computer and peripheral equipment manufacturing	12,940	$94,690
Computer system design and related services	12,760	$84,150
Architectural and engineering services	4,540	$88,520
Electronic instrument manufacturing	4,110	$84,580

■ **Top-paying states with number employed and annual mean wage**

State	Employment level	Annual mean wage
Colorado	2,870	$100,310
California	21,440	$94,560
New York	4,930	$92,890
Massachusetts	4,490	$92,700
New Hampshire	440	$92,350

■ **Most current numbers**—*www.bls.gov/oes/current/oes172061.htm*
■ **More information**—The Institute of Electrical and Electronics Engineers (IEEE) Computer Society, *www.computer.org*

How about a Power Trip?

Electrical engineers work with electricity in all its forms. They might figure out how to make your car's cruise control work better or how to keep the lights on in a building or in your community. They design, develop, test, and supervise the manufacturing of electrical equipment, systems, and components for industrial, commercial, scientific, or military use.

Electrical engineers differ from **electronics** engineers in that they generally focus on the generation and supply of power, dealing with large-scale electrical systems, while **electronics** engineers deal with small-scale systems. However, knowledge of both electrical engineering and electronics is useful in most electrical engineering work.

Electrical engineers design, develop, test, and supervise the manufacture of electrical equipment—such as electric motors, aircraft, automobiles, radar, and navigation systems, and machinery controls, lighting, and wiring in buildings. They may specialize in devices used by electric utilities to generate, control, and transmit power. They also may be involved in analog and digital telecommunications.

Note: Some universities consider **electrical** engineering to cover the **electronics** field, and **electronics** engineering graduates are sometimes called **electrical** engineers.

- **Cool things you can do**—Invent a new kind of computer processor; build dams to harness power; or make robots.
- **Specialty areas include**—Control engineering, power engineering, instrumentation, and telecommunications engineering.
- **Education**—Electrical engineers need a bachelor's degree. While some have degrees in advanced physics or electronics, most have electrical engineering degrees. There are 288 ABET-accredited electrical engineering bachelor's degree programs nationwide. Continuing education is essential to prevent technical skills from becoming obsolete.

- **Working**—Electrical engineers often work on teams with other engineers and scientists and can find jobs in industry, government, universities, or in consulting.
- **Average starting salaries in 2005**—Bachelor's—$51,888, master's—$64,416, and PhD—$80,206.
- **Employment outlook**—In 2005, there were 144,920 employed electrical engineers earning a mean annual income of $76,060. Electrical engineers comprise about 10 percent of the engineering workforce, but the number of graduating electrical engineers has fallen from a peak in the mid-1980s. Expect the number of job openings to be roughly equal to the number of graduates, with employment increasing an average amount of 9 to 17 percent through 2014. Strong demand for such electrical devices as wireless phone transmitters and large power generators should boost growth despite strong international competition.
- **Industries with highest levels of employment and annual mean wage (May 2005)**

Industry	Employment level	Annual mean wage
Architectural and engineering services	30,570	$75,420
Electronic instrument manufacturing	13,900	$79,110
Power generation and supply	11,360	$75,090
Semiconductor and electronic component manufacturing	10,620	$82,400
Scientific research and development devices	6,970	$82,710

- **Top-paying states with number employed and annual mean wage**

State	Employment level	Annual mean wage
Massachusetts	6,650	$85,750
California	18,840	$84,410
Texas	12,900	$84,180
District of Columbia	870	$83,260
Alaska	200	$83,260

- **Most current numbers**—*www.bls.gov/oes/current/oes172071.htm#nat*
- **More information**—Institute of Electrical and Electronics Engineers, *www.ieee.org*

Love Gadgets?

Electronics engineers make our televisions, radios, telephones, appliances, and even electronic games work better, to name just a few. They generally work with smaller systems than **electrical** engineers do, researching, designing, developing, testing, and supervising the manufacture of electronic components and systems.

They may use computer programs to help design electronic systems. Electronic engineers deal with devices that use electricity to control processes and also may work in areas related to computers (although engineers exclusively working with computer hardware are considered **computer hardware** engineers).

Almost one-third of all electronics engineers are employed by the telecommunications industry or the U.S. government.

- **Cool things you can do**—Invent a new kind of cell phone or TV; build video games; or invent micro robots to look inside the body to detect medical problems.
- **Specialty areas include**—Communications, power systems, computer engineering, microwave engineering, and digital signal processing.
- **Education**—Electronics engineers need a bachelor's degree. Some universities consider **electrical** engineering to cover

the **electronics** field, and **electronics** engineering graduates are sometimes called **electrical** engineers. There are 288 electrical engineering bachelor's degree programs accredited by ABET. Continuing education is important to prevent technical skills from becoming obsolete.

- **Working**—Several industries employ electronics engineers, including manufacturing, bioengineering, education and research, and aerospace.
- **Average starting salaries in 2005**—Bachelor's—$51,888, master's—$64,416, and PhD—$80,206.
- **Employment outlook**—In 2005, there were 130,050 employed electronics engineers earning a mean annual salary of $79,990. This field comprises about 10 percent of overall engineering employment. Expect jobs to increase as fast as the average, 9 to 17 percent, through 2014. Unfortunately, foreign electronics product development and engineering services will limit the rate of U.S. job growth. However, the situation should be helped by the increasing American demand for electronic products for consumers, industry, and defense. The largest area of job growth is expected to be in consulting firms that provide electronics engineering expertise.
- **Industries with highest levels of employment and annual mean wage (May 2005)**

Industry	Employment level	Annual mean wage
Federal government	18,700	$88,960
Semiconductor and electronic component manufacturing	15,700	$82,430
Wired telecommunications carriers	14,730	$72,250
Architectural and engineering services	9,450	$80,210
Electronic instrument manufacturing	9,300	$77,940

- **Top-paying states with number employed and annual mean wage**

State	Employment level	Annual mean wage
District of Columbia	1,130	$95,570
New Jersey	5,850	$91,690
Rhode Island	Unavailable	$90,840
California	25,290	$90,670
New Hampshire	930	$89,830

- **Most current numbers**—*www.bls.gov/oes/current/oes172072.htm*
- **More information**—Institute of Electrical and Electronics Engineers, *www.ieee.org*

Want to Protect the Environment?

Environmental engineers use the principles of biology and chemistry to solve environmental problems like water and air pollution, waste and wastewater treatment, and recycling.

They may deal with preventing, or cleaning up, pollutants that are biological, chemical, radioactive, thermal, or mechanical. Their work may include the use of technology for waste treatment, site remediation, and/or pollution control technology.

Environmental engineers sometimes use elements from civil, chemical, and mechanical engineering in their work. They design water supply and wastewater treatment systems, research the potential environmental impact of proposed construction projects, perform quality control checks, are involved in public health management and policy, and develop regulations to prevent hazardous waste problems and the methods to clean them up.

- **Cool things you can do**—Develop a plan for a national park; end pollution; figure out how to prevent acid rain; or clean up hazardous waste sites.

- **Specialty areas include**—Air-quality control, wastewater treatment, and toxic materials control.
- **Education**—A four-year college degree is required for most environmental engineering jobs. There are 55 ABET-accredited environmental engineering bachelor's degree programs, but some universities consider environmental engineering to be part of their degree programs in civil, mechanical, or chemical engineering.
- **Working**—With an interest in the environment, environmental engineers usually do some of their work outdoors. Many environmental engineers work as consultants to help clients follow regulations and/or clean up hazardous waste. One-fifth of environmental engineers work for the government at the local, state, or federal level.
- **Average starting salaries in 2005**—Bachelor's—$47,384.
- **Employment outlook**—In 2005, there were 50,140 employed environmental engineers earning a mean annual wage of $70,720. Expect this discipline to grow at a much faster rate than the average, increasing by 27 percent or more, through 2014 with more environmental engineers needed to comply with environmental regulations and also to find ways to clean up existing hazards. Public health concerns and a shift in emphasis toward preventing problems, rather than controlling them, also will result in more job opportunities.
- **Industries with highest levels of employment and annual mean wage (May 2005)**

Industry	Employment level	Annual mean wage
Architectural and engineering services	14,970	$70,690
Management and technical consulting services	8,500	$71,850
State government	6,210	$58,640
Federal government	4,060	$83,900
Local government	3,520	$65,340

- **Top-paying states with number employed and annual mean wage**

State	Employment level	Annual mean wage
New Mexico	380	$77,340
California	4,460	$76,840
Texas	2,270	$76,810
District of Columbia	1,700	$76,400
Washington	1,360	$74,860

- **Most current numbers**—*www.bls.gov/oes/current/oes172081.htm*
- **More information**—American Academy of Environmental Engineers, *www.aaee.net*

Safety First?

Health and safety engineers (except mining safety engineers and inspectors) make products and production processes as safe as possible. They promote worksite or product safety by identifying and measuring potential hazards to people and property.

They use their knowledge of industrial processes along with chemical, mechanical, and human performance principles to anticipate, recognize, and evaluate hazardous conditions and develop methods to control them.

- **Cool things you can do**—Prevent fires, nuclear accidents, or traffic accidents; make products safer; or help people avoid accidents at work.
- **Specialty areas include**—Industrial hygiene, construction, risk management/insurance, and public sector health and safety.

- **Education**—Most obtain four-year bachelor's degrees. Colleges generally offer a safety specialty within other engineering degree programs.
- **Working**—Some health and safety engineers work in industry to make sure the designs of new products will not create unnecessary hazards. Major areas of employment for health and safety engineers are manufacturing, service industries, construction, insurance, consulting firms, and the government.
- **Starting salaries**—About $40,000 with a bachelor's.
- **Employment outlook**—In 2005, there were 25,330 employed health and safety engineers earning a mean annual income of $67,240. Expect an average employment growth of about 9 to 17 percent through 2014. As concerns for health and safety in the workplace increase, and new technologies are developed, these engineers will be in demand.
- **Industries with highest levels of employment and annual mean wage (May 2005)**

Industry	Employment level	Annual mean wage
Federal government	2,620	$78,300
Nonresidential building construction	1,820	$61,420
Local government	1,450	$63,560
Architectural and engineering services	1,320	$80,240
State government	1,300	$57,000

- **Top-paying states with number employed and annual mean wage**

State	Employment level	Annual mean wage
Alaska	110	$93,110
Colorado	520	$81,650
District of Columbia	100	$81,400
Maryland	1,120	$79,930
New Jersey	770	$77,110

- **Most current numbers—**_www.bls.gov/oes/current/oes172111.htm_
- **More information—**American Society of Safety Engineers, _www.asse.org_

Want to Make Things More Efficient and Productive?

Industrial engineers figure out how to make and do things better. Some people think of them as "efficiency experts" or "productivity people."

Industrial engineers design, develop, and test methods to find the most effective way to use people, machines, materials, information, and energy to make a product or provide a service. They aim to increase productivity through management of people, technology, and business organization methods.

They are involved in such areas as plant location and/or layout, economical handling of raw materials, analyzing and planning jobs, and efficient inventory control. They may develop job evaluation programs or wage and salary administration systems. Industrial engineers may face such challenges as figuring out how to shorten waiting lines or distribute products across the globe.

- **Cool things you can do—**Figure out how to make stadiums and theme parks more people-friendly; make doctors and nurses more efficient; or help prevent lost luggage on airlines.
- **Specialty areas include—**Quality assurance/control, applied ergonomics, value engineering, and plant engineering.
- **Education—**Most industrial engineers have four-year college degrees. There are about 100 ABET-accredited industrial engineering degree programs and 26 specific manufacturing

engineering programs, but industrial engineers also may have degrees in mechanical, electrical, or computer engineering.

■ **Working**—With such versatile skills, industrial engineers can work in any kind of industry or organization, although most work for manufacturing or service companies. Because their work closely relates to the work of managers, industrial engineers often move into management positions. Industrial engineering also is sometimes called **operation management**. It is also referred to as **production, manufacturing, or manufacturing systems** engineering. In the health care field, industrial engineers are commonly known as **management** engineers or **health systems** engineers.

■ **Average starting salaries**—Bachelor's—$49,567, master's—$56,561, and PhD $85,000.

■ **Employment outlook**—In 2005, there were 191,640 employed industrial engineers earning a mean annual income of $68,500. Expect industrial engineers to have employment growth of 9 to 17 percent, considered about as fast as the average for all occupations, through the year 2014. Firms seeking to increase productivity and cut costs will increasingly turn to industrial engineers. In addition, many industrial engineers leave the occupation to become managers because the work is so similar, thus creating job opportunities.

■ **Industries with highest levels of employment and annual mean wage (May 2005)**

Industry	Employment level	Annual mean wage
Motor vehicle parts manufacturing	14,460	$65,460
Aerospace product and parts manufacturing	13,020	$68,080
Semiconductor and electronic component manufacturing	11,030	$74,250
Electronic instrument manufacturing	10,640	$73,500
Architectural and engineering services	9,360	$71,070

- **Top-paying states with number employed and annual mean wage**

State	Employment level	Annual mean wage
Alaska	80	$94,040
District of Columbia	Unavailable	$87,260
California	20,400	$79,300
Delaware	670	$79,270
Massachusetts	6,290	$75,150

- **Most current numbers**—*www.bls.gov/oes/current/oes172112.htm*
- **More information**—Institute of Industrial Engineers, *www.iienet.org*

What Floats Your Boat?

Marine and **ocean** engineers are involved in the design, construction, operation, and maintenance of structures in and around the water. Marine engineers generally deal with the propulsion, steering, and other machinery on marine structures ranging from underwater robots and oil rigs to submarines, tankers, and sailboats, and more. They also may design, operate, and/or maintain a vessel's mechanical, electrical, fluid, and control systems. Marine engineers also study engineering problems that face structures in the water, such as rust and environmental problems.

Ocean engineers study the ocean environment to determine its effects on marine vehicles and structures. They also may design and operate ocean platforms or deep sea exploration vehicles.

- **Cool things you can do**—Make submarines go faster; build robots to explore the deepest seas; design fancy yachts; or build giant oil rigs.
- **Specialty areas include**—Marine equipment design, marine equipment research, marine surveying, port engineering, and ocean structures.

- **Education—**There are only about 20 schools that offer degrees in naval architecture, marine engineering, and ocean engineering. People in this field are likely to have a background in hydrodynamics, material science, and mechanical, civil, and electrical engineering. Marine engineers also are familiar with ocean engineering.
- **Working—**Marine engineers work aboard ships and oil rigs, in shipyards, in traditional offices and sometimes a combination of all of these. Workers who maintain or supervise propulsion systems onboard vessels may be called ship or marine engineers even if they are not trained engineers, although most are.
- **Salaries—**Range from $43,790 to $109,190.
- **Employment outlook—**In 2005, there were 6,550 marine engineers and the overall mean annual wage was $74,320. Although this field is expected to experience slower than average growth of no more than 8 percent through 2014, there are a limited number of students pursuing careers in this discipline. Therefore, there will be job opportunities for those replacing workers who retire or take other jobs and for those able to profit from the strong demand for naval vessels, yachts, and other small craft. Expect this to more than offset the decline in the domestic design and construction of large ocean-going vessels.
- **Industries with highest levels of employment and annual mean wage (May 2005)**

Industry	Employment level	Annual mean wage
Architectural and engineering services	1,730	$66,580
Federal government	740	$89,960
Ship and boat building	620	$71,810
Other professional and technical services	540	$58,400
Support activities for water transportation	360	$73,840

- **Top-paying states with number employed and annual mean wage**

State	Employment level	Annual mean wage
Hawaii	80	$109,470
District of Columbia	260	$97,090
Maryland	320	$90,370
Michigan	Unavailable	$83,380
New York	Unavailable	$83,060

- **Most current numbers**—*www.bls.gov/oes/current/oes172121.htm*
- **More information**—Society of Naval Architects and Marine Engineers, *www.sname.org*

Want to Make Materials Better and Stronger?

Materials engineers develop, process, and test materials to create products. They study metals, ceramics, polymers (plastics), semiconductors, and combinations of materials called composites to see how they behave, find ways to use them to meet specific design requirements, develop new uses for them, or figure out how to improve the transfer of heat or energy.

Materials engineers study materials at an atomic level, using advanced processes that allow them to use computers to replicate the characteristics of the materials and their components.

- **Cool things you can do**—Improve athletic equipment; create a fabric to wear in space; use manmade materials to replace skin; or develop substances to move electricity better.
- **Specialty areas include**—Metallurgical, welding, mining safety, transportation, communications, and nuclear.
- **Education**—Materials engineers need a four-year college degree. There are more than 50 ABET-accredited bachelor's degree material engineering programs. However, some

materials engineers also have degrees in chemical or bio-medical engineering. The top research jobs, however, require at least a master's degree or a doctorate.

■ **Working**—Most materials engineers specialize in a particular type of material, such as metals (metallurgical), ceramics, plastics (polymers), semiconductors, and composites (combinations of materials). While the majority of materials engineers are involved in research and development for industry or at universities, expect consulting to become a growth area.

■ **Average starting salary in 2005**—$50,982 with a bachelor's.

■ **Employment outlook**—In 2005, there were 20,950 materials engineers earning a mean annual income of $71,390. The materials engineering field is expected to grow as fast as the average for all occupations, 9 to 17 percent, through 2014. Expect, also, growth to be particularly strong in the areas of nanomaterials (extraordinarily small materials) and biomaterials (synthetic materials to replace—or work with—part of a living system). An employment decline is expected in many of the manufacturing industries where materials engineers currently work, but there still will be a need to develop new materials for biotechnology, plastics, and electronics products.

■ **Industries with highest levels of employment and annual mean wage (May 2005)**

Industry	Employment level	Annual mean wage
Architectural and engineering services	1,900	$63,320
Aerospace product and parts manufacturing	1,800	$78,150
Semiconductor and electronic component manufacturing	1,650	$69,400
Scientific research and development devices	1,620	$81,350
Federal government	1,170	$92,520

- **Top-paying states with number employed and annual mean wage**

State	Employment level	Annual mean wage
Maryland	430	$89,400
Colorado	660	$83,770
Kansas	Unavailable	$80,700
Massachusetts	690	$78,990
Virginia	200	$78,460

- **Most current numbers**—*www.bls.gov/oes/current/oes172131.htm*
- **More information**—Minerals, Metals, & Materials Society, *www.tms.org*

Interested in How Things Work?

Mechanical engineers deal primarily with things that move. They research, develop, design, manufacture, and test all kinds of engines, tools, and machines.

They may oversee installation, operation, maintenance, and repair of equipment that produces power—like internal combustion engines, electric generators, and steam and gas turbines—or machines that consume power, such as equipment for refrigeration and air-conditioning, robots used in manufacturing, elevators and escalators, various heating and water systems, and industrial production equipment.

Mechanical engineering is considered to be one of the broadest areas of engineering and constitutes the second largest discipline after civil engineering.

- **Cool things you can do**—Design cars; work with lasers; build tiny machines to do big jobs; or find new areas to use robots.
- **Specialty areas include**—Automotive, biomechanics, energy, computer-aided design and application, petroleum technology, gas turbines, and processing.

- **Education**—Mechanical engineers need a bachelor's degree. There are almost 300 ABET-accredited programs that offer degrees in mechanical engineering.
- **Working**—Just about every company that manufactures a product also has a mechanical engineer. They work in all areas from research and development to production and maintenance. In addition, many mechanical engineers are managers or administrators.
- **Average starting salaries in 2005**—Bachelor's—$50,236, master's—$59,880, and PhD—$68,299.
- **Employment outlook**—In 2005, there were 220,750 mechanical engineers earning a mean annual wage of $70,000. Expect the mechanical engineering field to grow by 9 to 17 percent through 2014. The largest concentration currently is in manufacturing industries, where employment is expected to decline, but the demand for improved machinery and tools should increase the demand for mechanical engineers. In addition these engineers will be needed to deal with increasingly complex industrial machinery and processes. The biotechnology, materials science, and nanotechnology fields also will create new job opportunities. There will be other job possibilities because mechanical engineering skills often can be applied to other engineering disciplines.
- **Industries with highest levels of employment and annual mean wage (May 2005)**

Industry	Employment level	Annual mean wage
Architectural and engineering services	47,060	$73,690
Aerospace product and parts manufacturing	13,270	$75,090
Electronic instrument manufacturing	12,440	$74,440
Scientific research and development devices	10,660	$76,150
Federal government	9,720	$80,930

- **Top-paying states with number employed and annual mean wage**

State	Employment level	Annual mean wage
District of Columbia	600	$88,180
Delaware	580	$81,130
New Mexico	1,040	$79,170
New Jersey	5,590	$79,160
Alaska	380	$78,830

- **Most current numbers—**_www.bls.gov/oes/current/oes172141.htm_
- **More information—**The American Society of Mechanical Engineers, _www.asme.org_

What Riches Lie Under the Surface?

Mining and **geological engineers** (including **mining safety** engineers) are involved in the processes used to take minerals—from gold to gravel—from the ground. They find, extract, and prepare coal, metallic ores, and nonmetallic minerals (such as stone and gravel) for use by manufacturing industries and utilities. These engineers frequently specialize in the mining of one mineral or metal, such as coal or gold.

They design mines—both open-pit and underground—and related equipment, as well as supervise their construction and operation. They may also devise methods for getting the minerals to processing plants. **Mining engineers** also work to minimize the environmental effects of mining, such as changes to the land and water or air pollution. **Geological engineers** use the science of geology to study the earth and use engineering principles to find and develop deposits of natural resources.

- **Cool things you can do—**Discover gold and silver; develop new blasting techniques; or use satellite photos to find new mineral deposits.

- **Specialty areas—**Underground mining, surface mining, and mining equipment.
- **Education—**This type of engineering requires a bachelor's degree. There are 15 ABET-accredited bachelor's degree programs in mining engineering.
- **Working—**Due to the nature of this profession, most mining engineers work on-site.
- **Average starting salary in 2005—**$48,643 with a bachelor's.
- **Employment outlook—**In 2005, there were 5,650 mining and geological engineers employed in the United States and they were earning a median annual income of $75,070. Expect **mining** and **geological** engineers to have good employment opportunities, despite a projected decline in job growth through 2014 that will be in line with the expected decline in the coal, metal, and copper mining industries. Favorable employment opportunities will result from a combination of factors: relatively few schools offer mining engineering degrees so there is not expected to be a substantial increase in the number of annual graduates; many mining engineers are approaching retirement age; and there may be increased job opportunities worldwide as mining operations recruit U.S. graduates.
- **Industries with highest levels of employment and annual mean wage (May 2005)**

Industry	Employment level	Annual mean wage
Oil and gas extraction	1,220	$95,900
Architectural and engineering services	990	$63,380
Metal ore mining	690	$66,360
Coal mining	660	$69,470
Nonmetallic mineral mining and quarrying	370	$63,490

- **Top-paying states with number employed and annual mean wage**

State	Employment level	Annual mean wage
Maryland	Unavailable	$115,980
Texas	1,120	$93,200
Alaska	90	$85,450
Oklahoma	80	$85,070
Illinois	190	$80,430

- **Most current numbers**—*www.bls.gov/oes/current/oes172151.htm*
- **More information**—The Society for Mining, Metallurgy, and Exploration, *www.smenet.org*

Fond of Fusion?

Nuclear engineers develop methods, instruments, and systems that use radioactive materials and radiation for energy, medicine, and industry. They design, develop, monitor, and operate nuclear plants to generate power. They may work on the production, handling, and use of nuclear fuel and the safe disposal of nuclear waste, or they may work on the development of fusion energy.

Some nuclear engineers find industrial and medical uses for radioactive materials, as in equipment used to diagnose and treat medical problems.

- **Cool things you can do**—Invent new medical uses for radiation; develop ways to use radiation to produce and preserve foods; inspect nuclear power plants on the ground and on the sea aboard ships or submarines; or find ways to use nuclear energy to help space travelers go farther.
- **Specialty areas include**—Reactor operation, nuclear machinery testing, and food irradiation.

■ **Education**—Nuclear engineers need a bachelor's degree. There are about 20 ABET-accredited nuclear engineering bachelor's degree programs, but some nuclear engineers have advanced degrees in nuclear physics.

■ **Working**—Following safety procedures is essential to minimizing the risk of working with radioactive materials. No commercial nuclear power plants have been built in the United States for many years, but there will be a need to replace nuclear engineers who leave the field. Nuclear engineers also work in research and the medical fields.

■ **Average starting salaries in 2005**—Bachelor's—$51,182 and master's—$58,814.

■ **Employment outlook**—In 2005, there were 14,290 employed nuclear engineers earning a mean annual income of $90,690. Expect good job opportunities for nuclear engineers because the small number of nuclear engineering graduates is likely to be about the same as the number of job openings. However, job growth is expected to be only about 8 percent through 2014. Most openings will result from the need to replace nuclear engineers who transfer to other occupations or leave the labor force. Research and development of future power sources and new areas of medical technology may require nuclear engineers.

■ **Industries with highest levels of employment and annual mean wage (May 2005)**

Industry	Employment level	Annual mean wage
Power generation and supply	4,410	$88,830
Scientific research and development services	2,950	$91,860
Federal government	2,150	$87,230
Architectural and engineering services	1,950	$89,850
Employment services	80	$113,160

■ **Top-paying states with number employed and annual mean wage**

State	Employment level	Annual mean wage
Colorado	Unavailable	$138,970
District of Columbia	130	$124,700
Nevada	100	$114,190
Tennessee	650	$111,450
Maryland	290	$111,160

■ **Most current numbers**—*www.bls.gov/oes/current/oes172161.htm*
■ **More information**—American Nuclear Society, *www.ans.org*

Hunt the World for Black Gold

Petroleum engineers search the earth for oil or natural gas reservoirs. Then they work with geologists and other specialists to evaluate the potential of their find, figure out how to recover the most possible, and design ways to transport and store it. They supervise the construction and operation of oil and gas fields, and research new technologies to increase oil well and gas well production from the earth and beneath the sea.

Only a small portion of the oil and gas in a reservoir flows out under natural forces, so petroleum engineers use enhanced recovery methods such as injecting water, steam, chemicals, or gases to force out more of the oil and also do computer-controlled drilling or fracturing to connect a reservoir's larger area to a single well.

■ **Cool things you can do**—Travel around the world or create computer-simulated models to oversee multimillion-dollar drilling operations.
■ **Specialty areas include**—Drilling, production, and reservoir engineering.

- **Education**—A bachelor's degree is needed. There are 16 ABET-accredited petroleum engineering bachelor's degree programs available. Some petroleum engineers obtain geological engineering degrees.
- **Working**—Petroleum engineering offers the highest engineering starting salary. Although some work in labs or on computers, most work at oil and gas sites in the United States or abroad.
- **Average starting salaries in 2005**—Bachelor's—$61,516 and master's—$58,000.
- **Employment outlook**—In 2005, there were 14,860 petroleum engineers earning a median annual wage of $97,350. Expect the number of jobs to decline through 2014 because most of the potential U.S. areas for petroleum have already been explored. However, the number of openings from those leaving the discipline is expected to exceed the relatively small number of graduates. The best employment opportunities may be in foreign countries as many U.S. employers have overseas branches and many foreign employers want U.S.-trained petroleum engineers.
- **Industries with highest levels of employment and annual mean wage (May 2005)**

Industry	Employment level	Annual mean wage
Oil and gas extraction	7,280	$107,990
Support activities for mining	2,150	$80,150
Architectural and engineering services	1,400	$102,640
Petroleum and coal products manufacturing	810	$90,900
Management and technical consulting services	430	$91,000

- **Top-paying states with number employed and annual mean wage**

State	Employment level	Annual mean wage
Texas	7,610	$106,610
Alaska	220	$105,930
Ohio	300	$104,360
California	1,110	$94,200
Colorado	490	$93,430

- **Most current numbers**—*www.bls.gov/oes/current/oes172171.htm*
- **More information**—Society of Petroleum Engineers, *www.spe.org*

Other Areas

Here are a few other types of engineering that the U.S. government does not list as individual disciplines, and may consider to be specialties of the 17 main listings. However, they do have ABET-accredited college degree programs:

- **Architectural engineering**
  - Concerned with building issues
  - 15 ABET-accredited bachelor's degree programs
  - Generally considered a **civil engineering** subspecialty
  - For more information—*www.aeinstitute.org*
- **Ceramic engineering**
  - Convert materials into ceramic products
  - Six ABET-accredited bachelor's degree programs
  - Considered a **materials engineering** specialty area
  - For more information—*www.ceramics.org*
- **Construction engineering**
  - Plan and build buildings
  - Eight ABET-accredited bachelor's degree programs

- Generally considered a subspecialty of **civil engineering**
- For more information—*www.asce.org*
- **Engineering management**
  - Manage people working in technical jobs and the technological activities of an organization
  - 11 ABET-accredited bachelor's degree programs
  - For more information—*www.asem.org*
- **Engineering mechanics**
  - Involves the behavior of structural elements to loads
  - Eight ABET-accredited bachelor's degree programs, although engineering mechanics is more generally taught at the graduate level
  - Considered a subspecialty of **civil engineering**
  - For more information—*www.asce.org*
  - May also be considered a subspecialty of **mechanical** and **aerospace engineering**
- **Engineering physics**
  - An interdisciplinary area using math and physics to solve engineering problems, including superconductivity and applied thermodynamics
  - 30 **engineering physics** and **engineering science** ABET-accredited bachelor's degree programs
  - For more information—*www.aip.org*
- **Metallurgical engineering**
  - Dealing with metal-related areas
  - Three main branches of this area are physical metallurgy, extractive metallurgy, and mineral processing
  - 11 ABET-accredited bachelor's degree programs
  - Generally considered a subspecialty of **materials engineering**
  - For more information—*www.asminternational.org*
- **Optical engineering**
  - Combining optical theory, which deals with the properties of light, with engineering in the actual design and development of devices, measurement systems, and manufacturing processes
  - Two ABET-accredited bachelor's degree programs
  - For more information—*www.osa.org*

- **Survey engineering**
  - Determining the correct locations for projects
  - Seven ABET-accredited bachelor's degree programs
  - Generally considered a subspecialty of **civil engineering**
  - For more information—*www.asce.org*
- **Welding engineering**
  - Uses science and engineering to join components made of metal, ceramics, plastic, and other materials
  - One ABET-accredited bachelor's degree program
  - Considered a **mechanical engineering** subspecialty
  - For more information—*www.asme.org*

Okay, now you've had a taste of the possibilities that engineering offers. It's time to figure out whether you're already on the right path to reach one of them.

CHAPTER 4

Can Females Join?

You'll have to make your own turn

"Women are really good at this."
—Sherra Kerns, vice president for Innovation
and Research, Olin College

W e're not going to lie to you: It's not easy to be a woman in engineering.
You will be a minority in both the classroom and in the field. You may have to learn how to "talk boy" to survive. You also are likely to find yourself being a trailblazer at some point.

Nevertheless, the rewards will be worth it. You might even change the world.

"With absolute conviction I believe that there are amazing horizons to be met in the world of engineering and what it can bring to the fulfillment of a woman's life is huge," says Dr. Sherra Kerns, a national leader in engineering education and one of the world's top experts on preserving data in harsh environments.

"It's a boundless universe," she says.

However, most females don't seem to be aware of the possibilities. Even though women represent one-half of the students attending college, only about 20 percent of them study engineering. Moreover, when it comes to the workforce, the number of women plummets to somewhere around 10 percent.

There are many theories of why engineering is not more popular with females, ranging from a lack of role models to societal prejudices that also prompt high school guidance counselors to steer bright young women away from the field in favor of what they consider more appropriate—and often less academically demanding—courses of study.

But Kerns, vice president for Innovation and Research at trail-blazing Olin College, is not alone in believing that more females should choose engineering. "Women are really good at this. They're natural engineers—they're used to solving problems under the constraints of time, cost, and resources," she explains. "Women do this on a daily basis. They should be ideal for this."

So why aren't there more of them?

It's a question that has confounded educators, engineering organizations, and industry. They want more women engineering students on their campuses and more female engineers in the world. However, progress has been minimal, at best, in achieving those goals despite numerous initiatives to try to reverse the enormous under-representation of women and other minorities in engineering.

The Message Girls Get

Mary Mattis, the former senior program officer for the National Academy of Engineering's Diversity Program, says young women are essentially just as academically prepared for engineering as young men leaving high school, but "they just are not interested."

In fact, the Extraordinary Women Engineers Project, a recent initiative supported by the NAE and a coalition of societies representing more than 1 million engineers, found that girls are taking high school science and math classes at approximately the same rate as boys.

"The issue seems to be what we are communicating about what engineers do, or what we are not communicating," adds Mattis. "Women are getting a message of how hard it is to be an engineer and besides the geeky image, that all engineers do is sit at desks, drafting, and don't do things that change the world or help people."

Mattis says young women also are led to believe that engineering requires exceptional math skills, further exacerbating the problem for girls already "lacking in confidence in their ability to do math."

"It's not brain surgery becoming an engineer," Mattis says. "Women have the burden of having to be so much better than the norm in male-dominated professions. There are mediocre male engineers, as well as brilliant ones. We used to joke that we would know progress had been made when women are allowed to be mediocre engineers too."

Mattis says research by the Extraordinary Woman Engineers Project clearly demonstrated that "the messages we're sending to girls about engineering are not very appealing." The Project wants to reverse that by making girls understand the relevance of engineering.

"Now what we're trying to communicate about engineering is that it's a helping profession," says Mattis. "[The Project] has as its goal in the second phase to really go after . . . those who are academically prepared to go into engineering but choose not to."

Leann Yoder, executive director of the Junior Engineering and Technology Society (JETS), agrees that a new approach is necessary. "What's happening today is people are beginning to really focus on what's going to get a girl excited about engineering and that's very different from what's going to interest a guy.

"Girls are more interested in doing something that will fix a societal need, like getting water into a third-world country or cleaning up after Hurricane Katrina. Biomedical engineering is very popular with girls because they can help people."

Early Stereotyping?

Some people believe the problem goes far beyond the image of engineering, and may actually begin in the form of hundreds of small acts that begin at the youngest of ages, when groups of boys and girls are faced with the task of assembling something and it is the boys who aggressively step forward while the girls shyly step back.

If a girl is working on a project and fumbles a screwdriver, a boy will step forward to "help with that," truly believing he is doing her a favor. He's not. Dexterity with tools is a learned trait that girls can acquire as well as boys. Fathers (and mothers) tend to favor sons when it comes time for manual repair work and the tools of labor. Simultaneously, girls are introduced to kitchen chores and the tools of housework.

By the time girls and boys become young adults, the patterns are set. Males take center stage in the mechanical arts—building cars and buildings—while girls lean toward the human arts, such as nursing.

Those girls willing to defy the stereotypes to pursue engineering often find there are very few female role models among the predominantly male faculties and they will have to be willing to be an oddity in the classroom, as well.

Fortunately, there are on-campus support groups solely for female engineering students, such as the Society of Women Engineers or locally formed groups. Some campuses also belong to MentorNet, an e-mail mentoring network for female students and others underrepresented in the scientific and technical fields, which began as a Dartmouth project focusing on the retention of undergraduate women in engineering and the sciences.

In addition, female students have to deal with the issue of science education itself, which has been largely written by and for men. Even the projects most engineering students usually first take on have a decidedly male disposition—like rockets or four-wheel vehicles.

Betty Shanahan, executive director of the Society of Women Engineers, believes the problem is societal and it is society that is going to have to change. "In grade school, when a girl does well in math and science, we say, 'She works hard,' but when a boy does well, we say, 'He's skilled.'

"Well, how much fun is that for girls? To be told they have to 'work hard' to keep up with 'skilled' boys—when what's actually happened is that both have shown an aptitude for math and science and they should be encouraged equally."

Even as adults, she says, the patterns of a lifetime seem to be rigidly in place.

"I was in a group of engineers talking about a problem and the men kept jumping in with possible solutions. I'd start talking, only to have another colleague take over the conversation. Rather than assert myself, I'd step back—thinking I would get my turn to talk. But the truth is, women don't get a turn to talk. You have to make your own turn."

The NAE's Mattis also says, "engineering firms are not necessarily female-friendly," although there are some that are working diligently to change that.

Workplace Reality

Nevertheless, the statistics cannot be disputed. Remember that 20 percent of engineering undergraduates are female, but the representation of women among practicing engineers hovers around 10 percent. Why aren't they going into the workforce, or staying there?

Mattis believes it could be due to the fact that women, are "still the odd person out." In addition, she says, workplace advancement often requires work in field locations that "are not very attractive places for women, especially single women," frequent relocation, and a lack of family-friendly policies to retain and advance talented women engineers.

John MacGinnis, Chief Engineer for the Portsmouth Naval Shipyard employing 400 engineers in Kittery, Maine, says he has found that family considerations can be a factor in women leaving engineering.

"Almost half of the women we've hired that have come out of school in the past 15 years have left for that reason," he says.

Jamiyo Mack, an associate project manager with a large suburban Washington, D.C., consulting firm, says it can be a fear of the impact of such family considerations that also makes it difficult to be a woman in the male-dominated engineering profession.

"There are concerns that you might not be as dedicated to your job. I found that after I had my son, it was even more difficult. They were afraid I was going to have to leave early and such," Mack says.

Overall, however, SWE's Shanahan believes the engineering profession as a whole is improving in its efforts to make women and minorities feel welcome—mostly because efforts are being made earlier to identify anyone who seems to have an interest. "The problem is that as babies, we play with blocks and we're constantly trying to put things together and take things apart. But as soon as we get into school, we start reading about things instead of doing things.

"We need to encourage mechanical skills throughout education. There needs to be opportunity at every level to actually build things, fix things, and make better things."

Kathryn Gray, founder of GrayTech Software Inc. in Wheaton, Illinois, and president of the National Society of Professional Engineers, also believes things are changing for the better. "I'd say the treatment of women in engineering is improving. When you talk to women who became engineers 60 years ago, 40, 30, or 20 years ago, you find the closer they are to having graduated that there are less of the horror stories.

"There are still some disappointing stories out there about how women might be treated relative to men when it comes to promotions, pay, and selection as lead engineer for specific projects. Those difficulties still exist, but we are seeing less of them."

Cindy Wallis-Lage, Chief of Process Technology for the water division of the global engineering firm Black & Veatch, headquartered in Overland Park, Kansas, says that she has been fortunate in not experiencing problems related to her sex during her 19 years with the firm.

"There have there been a few occasions when I've been questioned, maybe, but only briefly. I didn't let it deter me. I proved myself and I ended up with very good relationships with people," says Wallis-Lage, an environmental health engineer for B&V Water. "What I don't like seeing is an exploitation of women—i.e., requirements that a project must have a woman or a minority on the job. I understand the basis for why it happens sometimes but when you're that woman, you don't like it. I'd rather be part of a project team on the merits of my ability and not on the basis of my gender."

Gray believes more of today's leaders are seeking the best person to do the job, regardless of their sex. The best advice for young women in engineering, she says, is to "be assertive and stand up for your rights."

"If there is a job that you are qualified to do and someone of the opposite sex equally or perhaps less qualified, gets the job, question why and don't be afraid," she says.

Resources

Here are some of the Internet resources available to explore engineering from the female perspective. The major societies also have divisions or committees devoted to women in engineering.

Celebration of Women in Engineering, *www.nae.edu/nae/cwe/ cwemain.nsf*, by the National Academy of Engineering defines itself as a "site for parents, teachers, engineers, and others interested in helping girls discover the opportunities in engineering careers."

The Engineer Girl Web site, *www.engineergirl.org*, is an offshoot initiative by the National Academy of Engineering to promote engineering directly to girls. It includes career information, games, and links to other sites.

The Extraordinary Women Engineers Project, *www.engineeringwomen.org*, is an awareness and outreach program designed to encourage young women to choose engineering as a career.

The National Women's Hall of Fame, *www.greatwomen.org*, has information on female engineers and other famous women.

The Society of Women Engineers, *www.swe.org*, has information about the engineering profession, career help, and educational programs for all ages. SWE has nearly 100 professional sections, 300 student sections, and members-at-large in all engineering and technology disciplines.

Women in Engineering Education, *www.engineering.tufts.edu*, offers career information, educational resources, a program database, and games.

The Women in Engineering Programs & Advocates Network (WEPAN), *www.wepan.org*, is a national nonprofit educational group with over 600 members from nearly 200 engineering schools, small businesses to Fortune 500 corporations, and non-profit organizations, all working for the full participation of women in engineering.

Engineering Wants You

Many colleges and universities want more female engineering students on their campuses and to get them there, they're actively recruiting young women and then trying to figure out how to keep them.

Engineering wants you. But are you right for it?

The self-assessment questions in Chapter 2 apply to both sexes, but if you have some of the qualities listed below, you might be an even better candidate than you realized:

- **You like to solve math and science problems**—You don't have to be a math or science star, but you should enjoy using your knowledge to solve math and science problems.
- **You think problems through**—Two important engineering skills are logic and analytical thinking.
- **You like being part of a team**—So much of engineering is done in teams that if you enjoy being part of a group effort, inside the classroom and out, engineering may be for you.
- **You like to look at things in a different way**—Creative and critical thinking are important in the engineering design process.

When it comes time to investigate potential engineering programs, ask questions that will help you get an idea of how female-friendly they are, such as:

- How many female engineering students are in the entire program?
- How many female faculty members are there?
- What is the percentage of female students enrolled annually?
- How many graduate and what is the percentage compared to male students?
- What is the percentage of job placement for females and how docs it compare to males?
- What groups are on campus to support female engineering students?

By the Numbers

The following information provides a snapshot of enrollment and degrees granted for women in engineering programs in the United States in 2005.

Undergraduate engineering degrees: 19.5%
Top discipline areas:
Environmental, biomedical, chemical, agricultural, and industrial/manufacturing
Most by school:
- Georgia Institute of Technology, 330
- University of Michigan, 285
- Pennsylvania State University, 266
- North Carolina State University, 255
- Purdue University, 228

Largest percentage to women:
- Yale University, 40.7%
- University of Puerto Rico, Mayaguez, 39.4%
- Tennessee State University, 38.6%
- Morgan State University, 36.7%
- North Carolina A&T State University, 36.6%

Engineering master's degrees: 22.7%
Top discipline areas:
Biomedical, environmental, architectural, agricultural, and chemical
Largest percentage to women:
- San Jose University, 49.8%
- Tulane University, 44.7%
- University of California, Santa Cruz, 44.2%
- University of Mississippi, 43.1%
- University of Notre Dame, 41.8%

Engineering doctoral degrees: 18.3%
Top discipline areas:
Biomedical, environmental, metallurgical and materials, chemical, and civil
Percentage to women:
- Tulane University, 40%
- Duke University, 38.5%
- University of Connecticut, 31%
- William Marsh Rice University, 30.8%
- University of Wisconsin, Madison, 30.7%

—American Society for Engineering Education

CHAPTER 5

Minorities: Getting to the Door

The importance of diversity

"Diversity is to creativity as innovation is to engineering."
—Linda P.B. Katehi, dean of engineering,
Purdue University

Engineering today is predominantly a white man's club and while the welcome mat is open for minorities to join, they are having a difficult time making it there. If you are a minority student considering engineering as a career path, and especially if you are Hispanic, African-American, or Native American, you most definitely will remain a minority in the workplace.

In fact, in each of the past ten years more foreign national engineers have been working in the United States than members of what are considered the under represented ethnic groups in the United States—Hispanic-American, African-American, and Native American engineers.

Only Asian-American engineers outnumber foreign nationals and even then, all these U.S. minority groups together remain little more than a blip on the engineering numbers radar and light years away from representing America's ethnic diversity.

Unfortunately, the situation isn't much better in most engineering classrooms, even if they are located on campuses that are home to students of all races:

- White males comprise nearly two-thirds of all U.S. engineering graduate and undergraduate students.
- U.S. minorities earn about 12 percent of the engineering undergraduate degrees awarded annually, a little over 5 percent of the master's degrees, and just 2 percent of doctorate degrees.
- About 61 percent of minority undergraduate students leave engineering before graduation.
- A large majority of engineering faculty members are Caucasian, compared to Hispanics and African-Americans, each at 2.3 percent of the total.
- The proportion of minority engineering college freshmen is declining compared to whites even though the number of minorities entering college is increasing.

These figures paint a fairly bleak picture when it comes to overall minority representation in engineering. Minority students concerned about the lack of diversity in engineering programs might want to consider attending a college or university with a larger general population of members of their ethnic group.

The historically black colleges and universities, for example, continue to produce the largest number of African-American engineering graduates. North Carolina Agricultural and Technical State University, Tennessee State, and Florida A&M University are among the HBCU schools that award a large number of engineering degrees.

Schools that have large Hispanic populations also dominate the production of Latino engineering graduates, such as the University of Puerto Rico, Poly University of Puerto Rico, and Florida International University.

The University of Oklahoma and Oklahoma State produced the most Native American engineering graduates in 2005, but together their number was only 37. The Tribal University and Colleges are working on an initiative to expand their engineering offerings, especially at the two-year pre-engineering level.

In total, California, Texas, and Florida produce the most engineering graduates from the underrepresented minority groups.

In the workplace, the electrical, mechanical, and chemical engineering fields are considered to be the most diverse but the number of minorities still remains extremely small in proportion.

It's not that minorities aren't wanted. It's just that people are having a difficult time removing the roadblocks preventing more of them from joining the profession. This creates issues on many levels, not the least of which is fairness.

However, diversity in engineering also is a necessity because the U.S. population is changing, with the overall number of minorities in the general workforce projected to increase significantly through 2012.

At the same time, the amount of white workers is expected to go up by just 8.5 percent. Compare that to an expected nearly 51 percent increase in the number of Asians, a 33 percent hike in Latino representation, and 19 percent more African-American workers. If engineering continues to be dominated by white males, who are themselves becoming a minority, there will be even fewer U.S. engineers in the future.

Then there are those who believe that diversity is a necessity for engineering to continue to create solutions to human problems. If we have only the white male perspective and the white males can't find the answer, then we all have a problem.

What Educators Think

"Diversity is to creativity as innovation is to engineering. Diversity is not just a responsibility, but also a way to achieve quality and leadership," Purdue Dean of Engineering Linda P.B. Katehi writes.

Dr. Sherra Kerns, a national leader in engineering education now serving as Olin College's vice president for Innovation and Research as well as a professor of electrical and computer engineering, says that engineering schools have begun to recognize the need for diversity.

"I think that engineering schools are starting to realize that in their enlightened educational self-interest they need to be more representative of the population," she says. "If engineers are to serve society, which they are—it's their job—they have to be able to appreciate the increasingly global and increasingly technological society.

"They need a variety of voices. Schools are becoming more active in efforts aimed at recruiting and retaining them. Not only are women and minorities coming in lower numbers, they're dropping out in higher numbers."

Kerns says schools are trying to reduce the barriers for women and minorities in the hope that once these students arrive on campus, they'll also no longer have to contend with any impression that they're there only because of their race or their sex.

The former National Academy of Engineering senior program officer for the Office of Diversity, Mary Mattis, agrees that despite numerous programs to increase diversity in engineering, "participation by minorities and women is declining." She is among those who believe the biggest roadblock is erected early in their school careers.

"The problem for minorities is that often they are not academically prepared," says Mattis. "They may be coming out of schools that don't even offer the kinds of courses that engineering schools expect."

The president of the National Action Council for Minorities in Engineering, Dr. John Brooks Slaughter, echoed similar sentiments in a 2005 address to NACME members:

"Minority students represent a significant resource pool for the engineering and technology workforce," Slaughter told the convention. However, he said, "of 659,000 minority high school graduates in 2003, only 26,000 had the requisite preparation in science and mathematics to qualify for admission to study engineering or technology at the college level."

Statistics indicate that students in schools with high minority populations are 40 percent more likely to be taught core academic subjects by teachers who didn't even minor in those subjects and students in very poor schools are 77 percent more likely to be taught by such teachers than students in less impoverished schools.

Even more disturbing is that even if minority students are fortunate enough to attend schools that provide them with strong math and science backgrounds, studies indicate that the very same teachers and guidance counselors who are overwhelmingly positive about engineering in the abstract believe that many of their minority students cannot succeed in the field.

What Students Think

Jamiyo Mack, a chemical engineer for a large suburban Washington, DC, engineering firm, was inspired by her high school chemistry teacher (also a female) to pursue engineering and decided to attend Florida A&M University.

"Coming from a predominantly black school they tried to make us realize as much as possible that the workplace does not look like where you go to school. It really prepared me for going out in industry," she says.

"They would talk to us about dress, appearance, and the importance of our written and oral communication skills," she says. "I also interned over the summers and I saw how corporate America worked."

Nonetheless, she says the predominantly white culture in the workplace can be difficult. Mack, as a member of the Society of Women Engineers and the National Society of Black Engineers, has been involved in engineering outreach efforts to inspire young minority students to become engineers. She says teachers especially tend to steer girls toward more traditional occupations but when girls have the opportunity to meet her and learn about her work, they become excited about engineering.

"Don't let people steer you," she advises minority students.

Diane E. Hodges Popps, a Native American who earned her master's in biomedical engineering and now works for Freescale Semiconductor in Texas, had been interested in science and technology since junior high but credits the MITES (Minority Introduction to Engineering and Science) program with her decision to apply to MIT.

Established in 1974 as part of a national effort sponsored by the then Engineers' Council for Professional Development, the rigorous six-week residential program on the MIT campus exposes promising minority high school juniors to engineering. Popps says of the 70 students who attended the MITES program with her, 30 ended up applying for undergraduate admission to MIT.

She says that while there are employers interested in recruiting minorities, her ethnic background did not get her a job. "I think that when companies are looking at hundreds of resumes, being a minority might open up the opportunity for a second look and an interview, but you have to prove yourself to get the job," Popps says.

She received several offers, but accepted one nine months before she started and based her decision on the diversity of the company. "It was important to me because of my background," she says.

Organizations and Societies

There are a number of organizations for minority engineers, and many of them have chapters on campus. Here are some of them:

The American Indian Science and Engineering Society (AISES), *www.aises.org*, was founded in 1977 by American Indian scientists, engineers, and educators concerned about the high dropout rates and low college enrollment rates of American Indian students compared to other ethnic groups. AISES has a variety of educational programs to offer financial, academic, and cultural support to American Indians and Alaska Natives from middle school through graduate school. It offers scholarships and has 160 college chapters nationwide, including 23 Tribal Colleges. Student membership is $25 annually.

Founded in 1974, the National Action Council for Minorities in Engineering (NACME), *www.nacme.org*, supports the effort to increase the representation of successful African-American, American Indian and Latino women and men in engineering and technology, math- and science-based careers. It is the nation's largest private source of scholarships for minorities in engineering. Since 1980, more than 17,000 students (nearly 15 percent of all minority engineering graduates) have received NACME support. It has campus chapters and K–12 resources, notably its *www.GuideMe-NACME.org* Web site that is of benefit to all pre-college students interested in engineering.

The National Association of Multicultural Engineering Program Advocates (NAMEPA), *www.namepa.org*, was formed in 1979 to increase the number of engineers from traditionally underrepresented minority groups (African-Americans, Hispanics, and American Indians). NAMEPA serves as an advocate for those students, promotes the professional development of members, and generally engages in a wide range of activities that respond to the needs of its membership.

The National Society of Black Engineers (NSBE), *www.nsbe.org*, claims to be the nation's largest student-managed organization with more than 10,000 members. It has 270 campus chapters, along with 75 pre-college chapters and 75 alumni extension chapters. NSBE has a pre-college initiative aimed at encouraging students in grades 6–12 to develop math and science interests and skills, as well as several programs at the undergraduate and graduate levels and a career center. Pre-college dues are $5; collegiate student dues are $10.

Established in 1973, the Society for Advancement of Chicanos and Native Americans in Science (SACNAS), *www.sacnas.org*, encourages Chicano/Latino and Native American students to pursue graduate education and obtain the advanced degrees necessary for science research, leadership, and teaching careers at all levels. It offers an e-Mentoring Program, online internship/job placement, a national conference, 15 student chapters, K–12 teacher workshops, and scholarships. Student membership is $24.

The Society of Hispanic Professional Engineers (SHPE), *www.shpe.org*, founded in 1974, now has 43 professional chapters and 179 student chapters across the United States and Puerto Rico. Through its Advancing Hispanic Excellence in Technology, Engineering, Math, and Science (AHETEMS) Foundation, SHPE offers K–12 outreach and scholarships. There is limited student information available to nonmembers on the Web site. The student fee is $5.

B**y the Numbers**

Here is a summary of engineering degrees granted by ethnic origin in 2005:

Undergraduate:
• Caucasian, 66.2%
• Asian-American, 14.1%
• Other, 8.6%
• Hispanic, 5.8%
• African-American, 5.3%

Master's:
• Caucasian, 58.3%
• Asian-American, 17.7%
• Other, 14.4%
• Hispanic, 5%
• African-American, 4.6%

PhD:
• Caucasian, 64%
• Asian-American, 14.4%
• Other, 14.2%
• African-American, 3.7%
• Hispanic, 3.7%
   —*American Society for Engineering Education*

The Society of Mexican American Engineers and Scientists (MAES), Inc., *www.maes-natl.org*, was founded in 1974 to increase the number of Mexican-Americans and other Hispanics in the technical and scientific fields. It has 18 professional chapters, 40 student chapters, and five high school clubs. It has K–12 outreach, undergraduate and graduate programs and scholarships, and job searching. The student fee is $10.

Also available at the graduate level is the GEM: Graduate Degrees for Minorities in Education and Science fellowship program, *www.gemfellowship.org*, designed to offer opportunities for underrepresented minority students to obtain master's of science degrees in engineering and PhD degrees in engineering and the natural and physical sciences through a program of paid summer internships and graduate financial assistance. Since its 1976 formation, it has brought together a consortium of companies and universities to provide graduate education to over 2,600 underrepresented minority students. Headquartered at the University of Notre Dame, it claims a master's in engineering graduation rate of 87 percent. It also offers pamphlets on success.

CHAPTER 6

The Pre-College Years

Making sure you're ready

*All parts should go together without forcing. You must remember
that the parts you are reassembling were disassembled by you.
Therefore, if you can't get them together again, there must be a
reason. By all means, do not use a hammer.*
          –Early IBM Maintenance Manual

W hat kind of education do you need before you get to
college?
          Lots of math and science. Have we said it often
enough yet? If you don't like math and science, step away from
this book because engineering will never, ever be right for you.

In 1817, the U.S. Military Academy at West Point became the
first school to offer an engineering education in America. Today,
there are hundreds of them, but one thing hasn't changed—every
one of them is based on a strong foundation in math and science.

"It's really when you marry mathematics with the physical sciences that you begin to separate the people who are going to be
successful in engineering from those who are not," says Dr. John
A. Weese, regents professor of engineering at Texas A&M University and former president of the American Society for Engineering Education.

Dr. Weese also believes a key indicator is whether a student
enjoys solving math puzzle problems. Those who do enjoy the
challenge tend to fit very well into a profession that is all about
problem-solving.

How early should future engineers begin building math and science skills? From the moment they first step into a kindergarten classroom, say some experts. Scores of engineering professional societies and organizations—and literally hundreds of colleges—have initiated K–12 engineering outreach programs. There also is a tremendous range of organized extracurricular engineering-related activities available to students of various ages and interests, ranging from competitions to build robots to ones that involve designing cities, and everything in between.

All of these efforts are intended to increase America's technology skills in general and even more specifically to expose children early enough to engineering so that more of them will choose the field that otherwise will be facing a true crisis by 2020 if more qualified American-born candidates are not attracted to it.

A few sobering statistics:

- The United States produces about 75,000 engineers annually. China and India each produce about 200,000.
- According to the National Science Board, the number of jobs requiring science and engineering training will continue to grow (currently by 5 percent per year compared to 1 percent growth in the rest of the labor force).
- Unless something changes quickly, however, the number of U.S. citizens prepared for these jobs will "at best, be level" because the children of an aging workforce are not choosing science and engineering in the same numbers as their parents.
- The people who will fill the nation's science and technology jobs 20 years from now are, like you, currently in school and trying to decide whether to study those fields.
- Meanwhile, the availability of people from other nations with the science and engineering training needed by U.S. industries will decline, either because of intense global competition for their skills or limits to entry to the United States imposed because of national security restrictions.

Obviously, there is room in the engineering field for you. The question is: how soon do you need to start thinking about whether you want to enter it so that you'll be ready?

"The earlier the better, obviously," says Dr. David N. Wormley, dean of engineering at Penn State.

"I think that you have to have in your mind that you would like to be an engineer when you are in high school," says the president-elect of the American Society for Engineering Education, "or you have to change your mind very quickly when you get to college, in order to take the right courses."

Some experts are convinced that making the decision as early as middle school is really best. They believe that's when you should begin building the foundation by taking courses, especially those in math and science, that will put you on the right college preparatory path.

Others believe high school is soon enough as long as you are in a college prep program because every college is going to require certain math and science classes for admission anyway. If you are short a few of the preferred number of math and science courses for an engineering education, it may not be an issue if you are otherwise a well-rounded and academically strong student. If need be, you could make up the difference through summer school or at a community college.

The experts all agree, however, that switching from being a dance or philosophy major to engineering at the end of your second year in college is probably going to be too late—unless you're prepared to add up to another four years to your college career in order to take all the courses necessary to earn a college engineering degree.

Whatever your situation, you should take to heart these words from Leann Yoder, executive director of JETS (Junior Engineering Technology Society):

"Engineering is about creating an idea in your head, thinking about it and making it happen," she says.

Yoder acknowledges that there has been a sense that if a student has not decided on engineering by 11th or 12th grade, it will be too late to get the necessary math and science classes to begin a college engineering program.

"A better approach is: 'it's too bad that you might not have taken the right math and science classes, but there's a way and let's map it out,'" she says. "High school educators often are not able to effectively counsel students about the diverse opportunities engineering study may provide and how best to prepare. Many educators think that students must be 'A'-students in both math and science to succeed in engineering and often that is not the case."

Yoder says community colleges can be an option for students to catch up or try a two-year engineering technology program that might inspire them to go for a full engineering degree.

"I believe that in this day and age, you can do anything if you have the passion for it."

Let's take a look at how to ensure that you're doing the right things to prepare just in case you end up deciding to pursue an engineering degree.

High School Preparation

Certainly, no two engineering programs are alike in terms of what they view as the ideal student.

If you already have a notion of where you might like to study engineering after high school graduation, be sure to check the institution's Web site—and specifically its engineering Web page—to see if you can learn more about the school's specific admission requirements and recommendations. If you can't find the information there, do not hesitate to contact the admissions office or the engineering program directly. (We'll talk more about choosing your institution of higher study in Chapter 7.)

If you think you already have narrowed down your engineering interest to one or two of the disciplines detailed in Chapter 3, check their professional organizations' Web sites. Many contain information on the types of preparation necessary to enter their specific field, both at the high school and college levels. Another excellent option is to find some real, live engineers in your community to talk with you about the profession.

If you haven't even thought that far ahead, don't be overly concerned right now. The most important thing you need to know is that engineering is a fairly rigorous course of study. You should be a pretty good student by the time you leave high school if you want to be successful studying engineering afterward.

Ideally, you would rank in the top third of your high school class upon graduation and should at least be in the top half. If you are in the bottom half of your class, engineering might not be a good choice for you. High school honors and advanced placement classes are optimal for any student who wants to study engineering in college.

An added benefit, according to a February 2006 study released by the Department of Education, is that completing academically challenging work at the high school level "dramatically" increases the likelihood of a student earning a bachelor's degree, regardless of the major.

You also should have fairly high scores on the math section of your aptitude test, whether you take the SAT or the ACT. Most engineering schools want to see a math SAT score of at least 550 and a total math and critical reading score of 1100, although the more competitive engineering schools prefer at least 1300 in the two categories, with 700 in math.

For the ACT, engineering colleges like to see a composite score of at least 28, with the math score ranking at 26 or higher, and the verbal at 24.

But don't despair if you don't fit these profiles.

"Many schools are now looking at a student's complete portfolio when they make decisions about admission," according to Dr. Wormley. "Some schools, and some of them are very good ones, no longer require SATs, although the majority still do."

As for coursework, the obvious math musts are Algebra I and II plus Geometry. You should take a fourth year of math. Consider trying Trigonometry. If you're really strong in math, go all the way and add Calculus.

On the science side, take four classes as well, including Chemistry and Physics.

Other courses of study helpful to a potential engineering student are computers (programming is a real plus) and electronics. If you're fortunate enough to go to a high school that offers engineering design or another engineering-based course, such as those available through the Project Lead The Way® program, absolutely take advantage of them.

Courses in graphics or design could be helpful because some engineers need to understand—or communicate—ideas or processes visually.

As with most professions, communication skills also are extremely important in engineering. Unfortunately, engineers do not have a good reputation in this area (we'll discuss that further in Chapter 18) but you might avoid the negative stereotype by taking classes or becoming involved in extracurricular activities that increase your writing and public speaking skills, such as debate or working on the school newspaper.

Don't forget that engineering is a global profession. Foreign languages, geography, and history will help you as well. To foster your creativity, classes in the arts and arts-related extracurricular activities are a bonus.

Another important skill for engineers is teamwork. You can learn a lot about that from sports and from being part of other student organizations or activities.

It's extremely important that you let your school guidance counselor know as soon as you do that you might be interested in engineering. Math and science classes build upon each other— you often have to take one before you can take another—so you need to get the basics in early in order to finish strong.

The last thing you want to have happen is to be a high school senior visiting the engineering program of your dreams and realize there is no way by graduation that you can complete the courses that your perfect college demands for admission.

Even if your high school does not offer all of the math and science classes we've listed, your guidance counselor should be able to help you make sure you have the rest of the bases covered and may know alternative routes to meeting your goal—such as taking a course at a nearby community college.

A little warning here: There is statistical evidence that indicates that (1) not all high school counselors truly understand what engineering is all about or the many disciplines it contains and (2) some counselors scare students into believing that engineering is "too difficult" and try to steer them away from the field.

This means you may have to take the lead by doing your own research, but as you do, take to heart the lessons of Chapter 2—almost anyone can be an engineer who:

- is a good math and science student,
- is curious and likes to solve problems, and
- wants to make something better in the world.

Meanwhile, be sure you take advantage of some of the many math and science activities out there that will help you learn more about engineering—and also indicate to any future engineering school your level of interest in the field.

Outside the Classroom

There are programs you can explore on your own via the Internet (*www.jets.org, www.discoverengineering.org,* and *www.k12engineering.org* have extensive lists) as well as programs you can do with others (see below for some possibilities).

You can even take family trips that center around engineering and science. Visits to science museums or the National Inventors Hall of Fame in Akron, Ohio, are obvious choices.

There are other engineering-related tourism opportunities out there as well. The National Society of Professional Engineers and National Engineers Week have even developed a Web site called "A Sightseer's Guide to Engineering" (*www.engineeringsights.org*), where you can click on a map of the United States and find a sampling of places to visit "that tell the engineering story." They are as varied as the Kennedy Space Center in Florida to the second largest electric shovel in the world in West Mineral, Kansas, and the Teton Flood Museum in Rexberg, Idaho.

The K–12 Engineering Center hosted by the American Society for Engineering Education at *www.engineeringk12.org* can be a good starting point for trying to find K–12 engineering outreach programs near you, as well as links to professional organizations and trade groups interested in K–12 outreach.

Here are just a few of the many other programs and competitions to consider joining or starting your own branch:

All Levels

The Future Scientists and Engineers of America (FSEA), a national nonprofit group, helps K–12 schools establish after-school technology clubs. Visit its Web site at *www.fsea.org*.

Science Olympiad holds academic interscholastic competitions with a series of individual and team events that follow the format of popular board games, TV shows, and athletic games. More than 14,000 schools nationwide participate in the four divisions: Grades K–3; 3–6; 6–9; and 9–12. More information is available at *www.soinc.org*.

In the ThinkQuest competition, sponsored by the Oracle Education Foundation, students work in teams to create the best educational Web sites. More than 30,000 students participate worldwide in the divisions: Age 12 and under; 15 and under; and 19 and under. Its Web site is *www.thinkquest.org*.

Elementary and Middle School

FIRST LEGO® League: For children ages 9–14, this is the "little league" of the FIRST Robotics Competition. During an eight-week program, children work alongside adult mentors to design, build, and program a robot to solve a real-world challenge using LEGO® MINDSTORMS™ Robotics Invention System™ technology. See *www.firstlegoleague.org* for more information.

Middle School

The National Engineers Week Future City Competition gives seventh- and eighth-grade students the opportunity to create cities of the future by first designing them using the SimCity video game and then making large tabletop models. Students work in teams with a teacher and a volunteer engineer mentor. More than 1,000 schools in 33 regions participate in this contest launched in 1993. The Web site is *www.futurecity.org*.

MATHCOUNTS® is a national math enrichment, coaching, and competition program that promotes mathematics achievement. Launched in 1983, more than 6,000 schools nationwide participate in the written and oral competitions held locally, with winners going on to state, regional, and national competitions. More information is available at *www.mathcounts.org.*

Middle and High School

The American Computer Science League organizes computer science contests and computer programming contests for junior and senior high school students. Begun in 1978, the ACSL has over 200 participating schools in the United States and Canada, as well as a few from Japan and Europe. Visit its Web site at *www.acsl.org.*

The BEST (Boosting Engineering, Science, and Technology) program, *www.bestinc.org*, gives student teams six weeks to work under the guidance of academic and professional coaches to design, build, and test a small radio-controlled robot for a robotics game based on an annual theme. Started in 1993, BEST has 8,000 middle and high school students participating in the contest.

Project Lead the Way® is a pre-engineering program now offered in over 1,300 middle and high schools in 45 states and the District of Columbia. Schools purchase the curriculum and agree to have teachers trained in the program. For more information, visit *www.pltw.org.*

In TechXplore, student teams work via the Internet with online mentors from consumer electronics, telecommunications, and high-tech companies to conduct research to solve a real world problem or address a quality of life issue. The research begins in early October and each team creates a Web site by the end of February to present its results. The National Science and Technology Educational Partnership sponsors this relatively new competition. Its Web site is *www.techxplore.org.*

High School Only

FIRST (For Inspiration and Recognition of Science and Technology) sponsors the FIRST Robotics Competition challenging high school students to work with professionals to design, assemble, and test a robot that can perform specified tasks in a competition with other teams. More than 70,000 students participate in the program founded in 1989 by Dean Kamen, inventor of the Segway Human Transporter. More information is available at *www.usfirst.org*.

The International Bridge Building Contest, *www.iit.edu/~hsbridge/*, based in Chicago, involves designing, building, and testing model bridges made of balsa wood to a set of specifications.

JETS (Junior Engineering Technical Society) is involved in three programs for high school students, along with the academic self-assessment NEAS+ mentioned in Chapter 2. JETS

- sponsors the annual TEAMS (Tests of Engineering Aptitude, Mathematics, and Science) program competition. Over 14,000 students participate in one-day competitions where they address engineering issues that represent college freshman-level engineering courses;
- sponsors the National Engineering Design Challenge (NEDC) where teams of students design, build, and demonstrate a working model of a new product to meet a societal need; and
- coordinates the U.S. Army UNITE (The Uninitiates' Introduction to Engineering Program) that helps prepare bright, talented, disadvantaged high school students and motivate them for success in engineering and technical careers through summer classes that show the connections between math and science and real world applications. It boasts a rate of 79 percent of its graduates enrolling in college.

More information on all three programs is available at *www.jets.org*.

Another Route—Engineering Technology

What if you haven't been the best student in high school but you still believe engineering is for you?

There is an option with less stringent admission requirements and an easier course of study that, in some states, can still lead to a Professional Engineer (PE) license.

That route is engineering technology.

Where an engineer is the team leader who develops the design of a project through drawings and specifications, the engineering technologist helps make the plans become a reality.

Two degrees are available: an associate's degree from a two-year program to be an "engineering technician" (less responsibility and pay) and a four-year option to be an "engineering technologist."

A technologist is the "applications" person on an engineering team, working with engineers during the initial design to make sure a project will do what it is supposed to do and will do it with available materials. Technologists often estimate the costs of a project and suggest the best ways to complete it.

A technician is the team's "doer" and troubleshooter, making sure the project works like it's supposed to. He or she is involved with its actual construction or manufacture, and with testing it afterward.

Two-year engineering technician degrees are available at technical institutes, community colleges, extension divisions of colleges and universities, vocational-technical schools, and through the military. Four-year technology degrees accredited by ABET are offered at about 230 universities and colleges. See *www.abet.org* to find one.

Few schools offer both degrees. If you decide to go the technician route with the hope of someday being a technologist, make sure the credits from one program are transferable to the other.

It also is extremely difficult to transfer engineering technology credits to a full engineering degree. The first two years of an engineering degree involve challenging and lecture-based math and science courses. In engineering technology, there is an equal amount of hands-on learning and lecture classes.

To pursue a four-year technology degree, you still need college-preparatory math (at least two years of algebra and geometry) and science classes in high school. Technologists spend a lot of time working with computers, so courses in computers, drafting, and other technical applications would be helpful. They also read complex materials and write about their work, so English and communications skills are important.

However, honors and advanced placement classes are not necessary for entrance into a four-year engineering technology program. Standardized test scores also need not be as high as for engineering. However, you should still take advantage of technology-related extracurricular activities to explore the field while still in high school.

On campus, engineering technology students typically major in a specific discipline, just like in engineering, and the opportunities are similar. Electrical/electronics, mechanical, and general engineering technology are the most popular areas. Others are construction, industrial/manufacturing, architectural, and computer engineering technology. Only certain schools offer more specialized areas, such as telecommunications engineering technology.

Engineering technology has its own honor society, Tau Alpha Pi, and engineering technology students and graduates are welcomed into major engineering organizations. (See Chapter 9 for more on societies.)

Some states allow engineering technology graduates from ABET-accredited programs to take the Professional Engineer exam, but may require more than the typical four years of experience that engineering graduates must have under the supervision of a licensed PE. Other states will not, but licensing is not mandatory in all engineering jobs anyway.

After graduation, you'll find there are more than a half-million engineering technicians and technologists—one-third of them in the electrical/electronics field. Median salaries range from about $40,000 in the civil and environmental disciplines to $52,500 in aerospace. The government expects employment to grow as fast as the average for all jobs through 2014.

For more information about engineering technology, check the Web sites of the various engineering societies or *www.eteducation.org.*

CHAPTER 7

Time to Think about Higher Education

Things to consider, choices to make

"We were shepherded in for our first lecture on engineering drawing ... There we were confronted by the lecturer, a Mr. Rawlinson, an elderly gentleman with a nicotine-stained moustache. He looked around the room at us and then said, 'I know your lot. Your parents said, Our Jim's not very bright in the head but he's good with his hands, so we'll make him an engineer.'"

–Frank Vann on his first day at University College Nottingham, 1941

You think that you might want to pursue an engineering degree, and you're on track to get the high school courses most engineering programs want to see on your transcript.

What's the next step to make sure you're among the approximately 97,000 freshmen who enroll in college engineering programs every fall?

Is there anything you can do now to increase the likelihood that you're eventually among the approximately 73,000 students who earn bachelor's degrees in an engineering discipline each year?

The simplest answer is: Choose wisely.

Invest some time thinking about the type of engineering you want to study and whether it truly fits your personality. That will help you figure out the next step of determining the best place to study it.

Don't despair if you're already stuck on Step 1, even after reading Chapter 3 and doing your own research. You're not alone. In fact, the problem is so common that a University of Maryland mechanical engineer has developed a software program to try to solve it. (See the item at the end of this chapter.) In addition, you should be aware that there are general engineering degrees available.

Furthermore, most engineering programs do not require you to choose a specialty until the end of your sophomore year or the beginning of your junior year. You are going to spend the greater part of your first two years taking prerequisite courses potentially usable for most any engineering major, including an overview of engineering in general, so you still have time.

However, we should note here that some engineering educators believe this theoretical type of curriculum may be to blame for the relatively high engineering program dropout rate. Some schools are instituting hands-on engineering programs earlier in the process to retain students who otherwise would become frustrated with two years of mostly theoretical study.

You also might want to give some thought to what you intend to do with your degree:

- Do you plan to get a job right out of college?
- Will you continue on with graduate school in the field of engineering (recommended for some disciplines) or pursue another higher degree, like medicine or law (not uncommon)?
- Have you considered high-level research or teaching at the college level, which requires a doctorate degree?

The answers to these questions, or the way you're leaning on each of them, could be a factor in your decision-making, especially if you are considering pursuing a graduate-level degree and think you might prefer to remain on the same campus. In addition, some undergraduate engineering programs focus on taking their graduates in a single direction, such as readying them for the workplace or preparing them for research and advanced degrees.

Once you've decided which engineering direction to take, or even if you haven't, you'll need to concentrate some time and effort on finding the type of program that will give you the best opportunity for success—both in school and afterward. There are hundreds of engineering curriculums out there. One of them is bound to be a good choice for you. At any given time, there are more than 370,000 full-time students studying engineering.

You want to be part of that crowd, not with the large number of engineering students that end up dropping out of the field completely.

Step 1—Choosing a Discipline, If You Can

It will be easier to move on to Step 2, choosing where to study engineering, if you already have completed Step 1 of generally deciding which type of engineering to study. All schools do not offer every type of engineering.

There are five major engineering disciplines that account for about 80 percent of the engineering bachelor's degrees awarded—mechanical, electrical, civil, chemical, and industrial. If you are unsure which one is for you, try to pick a school that offers all of these major disciplines so you won't have to transfer later. However, some disciplines—like ocean or forest engineering—are only taught at a limited number of institutions. Selecting a smaller discipline will narrow your higher education choices.

Hopefully, at least one or two of the many types of engineering described in Chapter 3 appealed to you. Knowing your areas of interest will help you find a school that offers degrees in them, and go a long way toward making your experience a positive one in the face of engineering's demanding curriculum.

"The real key to success is to find an area that they are really intrinsically excited about so they will be willing to put the work into it," says Dr. David N. Wormley, Penn State's dean of engineering.

Whether you find that exciting field before you even begin studying engineering, or two years into it, it will be up to you to actively search it out.

"You don't want to sit there and hope that by osmosis something happens," says Texas A&M University regents professor John A. Weese. "You've got to be actively thinking about it: about what turns you on and what does not.

"Most of the time students come in with an idea of what they are going to major in. People can move from one program to another. But usually people have some idea of what kind of technical devices appeal to them. They can certainly distinguish between things that are mechanical, like engines, versus things that are electronic, for example," he says.

It is not uncommon for accepted engineering students to change their minds about their preferred discipline after they arrive on campus and because the first two years are heavy on math and science, you still will have time to change your mind (more on this in the next chapter).

Step 2—Choosing a School

Most engineering jobs require at least a bachelor's degree, which the majority of engineering students obtain in four or five years. Beyond that, there are few additional basics you should know:

1. Some schools offer a Bachelor's of Engineering (BE) while others award a BS, or Bachelor's of Science, in engineering. The title of the degree is a matter of preference by the institution as there is no difference between them.
2. You have a choice when it comes to picking the type of higher education institution to seek an engineering degree:
   - *Polytechnic institutes* or *institutes of technology* are well-known for their engineering and science programs. However, if you're unsure about engineering, you might

want to consider another type of school that provides an opportunity to transfer to a non-science major.

- *Universities* are large schools offering a wide variety of majors. They have one administration overseeing different "colleges," such as engineering.
- *Four-year colleges* generally are smaller than universities. Their engineering programs may include more liberal arts emphasis.
- *Co-op programs* are five to six years long, but they provide a valuable opportunity for engineering students to truly experience the engineering profession while gaining valuable workplace experience even though they are still students. You would attend classes part of the time and then work in an engineering-related job for the remainder.
- The *military academies*—Air Force, Coast Guard, Merchant Marine, Military, Army, and Naval—require students to serve in the armed forces after graduation as payment for receiving an engineering degree at minimal or no cost.
- *Community* or *two-year colleges* offer pre-engineering courses that allow students to begin studying engineering at smaller schools with lower tuition and less stringent admission requirements. They also may award an associate's degree in engineering. You should make sure that the credits obtained from a community college or two-year college will be accepted by an engineering program at the four-year school you ultimately choose. Some community or two-year colleges have such written agreements with local four-year institutions.

3. Not every engineering program has been accredited by ABET, the Accreditation Board for Engineering and Technology. Established in 1932, ABET is a federation of professional and technical societies that collaborates on developing standards for accreditation. ABET is the recognized U.S. accreditor for post-secondary programs in engineering, as well as for programs in applied science, technology, and computing.

Most states require you to have a degree from an ABET-accredited engineering program in order to eventually sit for the exams that lead to the title of Professional Engineer (PE). If you want to have that option later, choosing a school with an ABET-accredited program is especially important. Chapter 14 provides more information on the PE exam and licensing.

About 350 colleges and universities in the United States offer at least one ABET-accredited engineering program. Most engineering programs at the baccalaureate level do seek ABET accreditation, but about 3 percent are new and not yet eligible or have elected not to be accredited by ABET.

For most of its history, ABET had extremely specific standards for accreditation, in some cases down to the number of credit hours in various topics and covering three-fourths of the curriculum, which limited program innovations along with the electives an engineering student could take. As of 2001, however, all of the four-year bachelor's degree programs were following requirements that focused more on what students learned and less on what was taught. Engineering programs stated their goals for students to attain certain abilities and knowledge, along with required levels of proficiency.

"The focus is more on program outcomes and educational objectives that are linked to the mission of the institution and the program," says Kathryn Aberle, ABET associate executive director. "Now we say, 'Tell us what it is students are expected to know and be able to do and what are your expected accomplishments for your student graduates? We want to know have you met those and if you have not, what are you doing to improve?'"

While this means that a mechanical engineering program at one university no longer is nearly identical to one at another, it provides more program diversity to meet a student's particular goals. It also responds to a trend in the lines being blurred between engineering disciplines.

"In some areas, there aren't those specific disciplinary boundaries but that is also where exciting things are taking place," says Aberle. "One area is bioengineering, where you have a convergence of the biological and engineering sciences."

You can search for accredited programs on the ABET Web site, *www.abet.org*, by region, discipline, and state, or a combination. The ABET site will provide you with direct links to the schools' Web sites. In addition, do not hesitate to contact the schools directly to learn even more about their programs.

To get an idea of the types of ABET-accredited engineering degree programs, consider this 2006 list by discipline:

Aerospace (61)
Agricultural (40)
Architectural (15)
Bioengineering (36)
Ceramic (6)
Chemical (156)
Civil (193)
Computer (174)
Construction (8)
Electrical (288)
Engineering (General) (35)
Engineering Management (11)
Engineering Mechanics (8)
Engineering Physics/Engineering Science (30)
Environmental (55)
Forest (3)
Geological (16)
Industrial (99)
Manufacturing (26)
Materials (52)
Mechanical (298)
Metallurgical (11)
Mining (15)

Naval Architecture & Marine (9)
Nuclear (19)
Ocean (9)
Other:
Fiber Engineering (2)
Fire Protection Engineering (1-U. of MD, College Park)
Optical Engineering (2)
Paper Science Engineering (3)
Structural Engineering (1-U of Calif., San Diego)
Systems Engineering (10)
Textile Engineering (4)
Transportation Engineering (1-U. of Arkansas)
Petroleum (16)
Plastics (1-U. Mass-Lowell)
Software (10)
Surveying (7)
Welding (1-Ohio State)

The American Society for Engineering Education provides profile information on a number of schools offering engineering degrees that potential students will find helpful (including costs to attend, ratios of students to instructors, whether they also offer graduate degrees, and statistical information about accepted freshmen) on its Web site, *www.asee.org*, and also sells the information in book form. Be aware that the schools, not an independent third party, provide the information. A less detailed search function can be found at the group's Web site *www.engineeringk12.org*. Many of the engineering groups representing specific disciplines also list schools that offer degree programs in their areas.

Now that you're aware of the basics, you should first evaluate schools by the same standards you would use no matter what your major: Do you want a small school or a large one?

Do you want a large engineering program? Penn State awarded 1,396 bachelor's degrees in engineering in 2005, followed by Georgia Institute of Technology at 1,372; Purdue with 1,261; North Carolina State University with 1,240; and the University of Illinois, Urbana-Champaign, with 1,198.

At the other end of the scale were schools like Southeast Missouri State University that awarded just two bachelor's degrees in engineering, Monmouth University and the University of Bridgeport that each awarded four, and Philadelphia University, Carroll College, and the University of Arkansas at Little Rock that all awarded just six engineering bachelor's degrees.

Other issues to consider: How big are the classes? Do you like the city or country? Is in-state tuition a factor? Is diversity among the student body and/or faculty important to you? How much of an academic challenge are you ready to take on? Are you academically prepared to compete in the classroom with the other students? What are their average grades and SAT or ACT scores? Are there tutoring services and study groups to help you?

Once you've answered those questions and narrowed your list accordingly, you should think about some criteria that are specific to an engineering education:

- How soon will you actually study engineering, and how much of your first two years will be dedicated to math and science theory?

- How much engineering creativity is encouraged in the classroom?
- How useful will your work be—will there be real-world applications?
- How accessible is the engineering faculty?
- What kind of support is available for you to make sure you succeed by providing such opportunities as internships, mentors, and/or student chapters of professional societies on campus?
- What kind of research are the faculty and graduate students involved in? Will there be an opportunity for you to participate as an underclassman?
- Does the school sponsor engineering-related events, such as design competitions and guest speakers?
- How will the school help you find a job?

What is its placement rate for engineering jobs upon graduation?

These are all things to consider when you're trying to decide where to study engineering.

Check the various sources that rank colleges, such as *U.S. News and World Report* or the Princeton Review, for more information on top engineering schools. You also can learn about a school by visiting its Web site or by requesting information from its admissions office.

These steps generally precede making a physical visit to the campus, which is vitally important before you plunk down a tuition deposit. Along with taking a general tour to get a feel for the school, try to arrange an interview with someone in the engineering department. Seeing the engineering classrooms and sitting down and asking your questions face-to-face will prove to be invaluable. Also try to speak with some current engineering program students to learn more about the program from their viewpoints.

You should choose an engineering program with the same methodical and logical way of thinking that will make you good at this profession.

A Tool for Discovering Your Path

Even as students are considering a career in engineering, a new tool is becoming available that not only will help inform them about the career from an early age, but also help identify their likelihood of success in specific disciplines of the profession.

Even better, the testing is done on a computer and results are almost instantaneous, rather than with pencil, paper, and waiting three weeks to get them back. The software is "Pathevo" (for Path Evolution), produced by the Owen Software Development Corporation in Rockville, Maryland.

Software developer Adeboyejo Oni, a PhD mechanical engineer and CEO of Owen Software, says, "Part of the problem is that even middle school counselors don't really understand what engineers do, and they don't know how many different kinds of engineers there are."

Dr. Oni notes that few middle school or high school counselors actually have engineering degrees and therefore are hard-pressed to recommend education paths that they know so little about. Moreover, in public schools there may be as many as 500 to 600 students per counselor.

"Even if they (counselors) know the basics of engineering, they usually don't know a lot about subdisciplines like robotics, thermal dynamics, design, fluid engineering, and other segments of the profession," he says.

It's hard to help students if you don't know where to send them. To help fill that void, at the middle school level Pathevo allows students to sit at a computer and explore the company's Web-enabled application, where more than 1,500 video clips are available on almost every kind of engineering you can imagine.

"That way, students can explore on their own and the counselors don't have to answer questions they may not be comfortable answering," Dr. Oni says.

If a middle school student displays an interest in a discipline, then both the counselor and parents can discuss appropriate coursework for the future. At the high school level, Pathevo provides an online aptitude testing site that can give a student feedback immediately on his or her chances of success as an engineer.

"One of the things we found was that students don't like paper and pencil tests. This is the computer age and students want to take tests on computers—and they want to know the results right way, rather than wait weeks to find out."

Dr. Oni says the Pathevo software can even help nudge a student toward certain engineering disciplines where achievement appears more likely.

Once a high school student discovers whether he or she is likely to be a successful engineering student, the search can begin for an appropriate college. Of key importance is that the software is broadly based. Just because a student does well in math and science doesn't necessarily mean he or she is cut out to be an engineer.

"Math and science are important, but they are just part of what makes a successful engineering student. Our software tries to look at the entire person," Dr. Oni says. "You'd be surprised at how many college engineering students—getting good grades and doing well—suddenly decide after their second year that they want to do something else.

"Emotions run high. Parents worry that they've wasted thousands of dollars. The software tries to measure a lot of things about the student, including whether they would be happy in an engineering career."

In some engineering disciplines, Dr. Oni says, even math and science skills need not be exceptional. "Design engineering, for instance," he says. "You can be average in math but if you can express yourself through artistic shapes, you could be an excellent design engineer and work for one of the big auto makers designing cars. You would see things differently than math or science students would see them.

"You have the same thing in designing buildings. You could miss the aesthetic focus if you rely too heavily on just the mathematics of construction."

Currently, the Pathevo data is licensed to schools for use. Dr. Oni is optimistic, however, that someday the government will underwrite the test and provide it to schools free.

CHAPTER 8

On the Campus

How to defy the odds

*"Every semester there's one class that's
ridiculously hard. You just have to bear it."*
—Michael Allen, engineering student

O nce you've made it into an engineering school, it may
be important to remember why this was a good idea. As
you take on the challenge of studying engineering over
the next four, five, or however many years, your motivation will
be a major incentive helping you defy the odds and earn an engineering diploma.

Remember those high dropout numbers for engineering programs? You want to find a way not to be one of them. You can do
it—and it will help if you keep in mind the rewards of an engineering education.

"I tell people who think they may have an interest in engineering that an engineering program is a very satisfying thing to
study," advises John Weese, a former engineering dean now
regents professor of mechanical engineering at Texas A&M.

"At the end of every semester, you will have learned things that
are useful, things that you can apply and things you didn't know
at the beginning," he notes. "It's a lot of work and it tends to be a
heavy course load. But it also tends to be more fun than a lot of
things and it's very rewarding because you have a constant feeling
of moving ahead."

Why Students Leave

Why do so many students walk away from engineering?

"There are some statistics that show a dropout rate of around 50 percent but one thing is that engineering is very challenging. Students have to work very hard," says Dr. David A. Wormley, Penn State's dean of engineering and the president-elect of the American Society for Engineering Education.

Sometimes it's a matter of engineering students arriving on campus without a clear understanding of the profession, or the amount and type of coursework required to be successful. (They haven't read this book.)

"Part of the reason kids fall out of engineering is they get to college and they have no idea what it's about," says JETS Executive Director Leann Yoder. "Engineering is really about taking a concept and trying it over and over again until you get it right."

In addition, in the first two years most engineering curriculums are heavy on math and science classes—and extremely light on any engineering, no matter which discipline you choose.

"The first two years were mostly physics and math. They don't give you any real world application of them until you get to the engineering classes," agrees Michael Allen, a University of Connecticut junior studying management and engineering for manufacturing.

"Every semester there's one class that's ridiculously hard. You just have to bear it," he says. "They try to get people out of the major by having it, to make people think whether they really want it."

In the second two years of an engineering program, you concentrate on your chosen discipline, although the practice of engineering is becoming so interdisciplinary that you also may take courses that traditionally fall within other majors. No matter which area you choose, though, engineering will be academically challenging.

"They need to be reasonably well organized," Penn State's Wormley says. "They do need to be pretty bright and they need to be able to work very hard."

Wormley notes that college students in every major often change direction, and may do so two or three times before they settle on one. However, he says this trend isn't as obvious in areas like liberal arts, where students change majors and still remain within the broader liberal arts curriculum. He also is among many educators who believe that a major contributing factor to the engineering campus exodus has been the frustration of students over a lack of engineering in their first two years of study for the profession.

"They have no contact, or very little contact, with engineering itself," he says. "But now, many colleges are changing that."

He says Penn State now has a required freshman engineering course that addresses creativity and teamwork in engineering. Other schools offer freshman seminars that discuss how to deal with environmental problems from an engineering perspective. Some institutions have classes early in the curriculum that expose students to the various types of engineering, allowing for the possibility that a student might change his or her chosen engineering discipline.

There also are efforts to concentrate more on ethics, sustainability, business skills, and ways to improve the communication skills of engineering students at some point during their education.

What's still missing is interdisciplinary learning in the undergraduate engineering curriculum, according to a 2005 National Academy of Engineering report that concluded today's engineering students may not be adequately educated to meet the demands that will be made of their profession in 2020.

According to the Academy, interdisciplinary teams now play a larger role in industry, government laboratories, and academic institutions, but this type of learning does not usually show up in engineering education until the graduate level. The report said undergraduate engineering programs need to be "reshaped" to attract students to engineering, prepare them to compete in the global marketplace "and ensure that America's pre-eminence in engineering is not lost."

ABET, the Accreditation Board for Engineering and Technology, requires that accredited programs find ways to make sure students attain certain general engineering abilities and specific proficiencies for each discipline, but leaves the "how" and "when" up to the schools.

However, most first- and second-year engineering students spend the vast majority of their time in lecture-based courses designed to provide them with a thorough understanding of the principles and theory of math and science necessary for engineering design.

"The way in which we often teach engineering is: difficult, dry, and dull," says Dr. Sherra E. Kerns, an ABET evaluation team leader who has been an engineering educator on four college campuses, most recently at the innovative Franklin W. Olin College of Engineering (see page 108).

"But that's not necessary. It can be inspirational. Engineering problems all have more than one solution," says Kerns, citing engineering's creative aspect. "Sometimes it seems as if there is an embedded sense that if it's not painful, then you must not be providing an appropriate education."

Keith Morris, who received an undergraduate degree from Rensselaer Polytechnic Institute and his master's from MIT, is among those who believe there is an ulterior motive.

"The first two years are tremendously theoretical, boring, and difficult, but I think engineering schools purposely use that to weed out lots of people," says Morris, now president of ATI Industrial Automation in Apex, North Carolina.

Strategies for Staying

So what do you do if you find yourself in a "painful" or "difficult" program? Again, remind yourself why you chose engineering in the first place. If you can get through the first two years, you'll be well on your way.

Seek out on-campus tutors and talk to upperclassmen who can provide insight into the stimulating engineering courses ahead. Visit with your advisor for advice on how to cope. You will not be the only engineering student who has wanted to give up.

(Remember that 50 percent figure?) Engineering schools want to find ways to make you stay.

Take advantage of valuable peer support and networking through the various student engineering chapters and clubs on every campus. (See Chapter 9 for more on these groups that offer a variety of ways to immerse yourself in engineering, including tours, activities, networking, and speakers.) Every discipline's national organization has campus chapters, and there also are groups solely for women and minorities.

Get involved in engineering research projects on campus. Check with your advisor or engineering dean for possibilities. Don't ignore the exciting competitions offered by national engineering organizations and other groups, like the Department of Energy's contests to build solar-powered cars or homes, or the National Inventors Hall of Fame "Collegiate Inventors Competition."

Join campus chapter outreach efforts to younger students. It will help remind you why engineering is such a stimulating career option. Also, don't hesitate to reach out to practicing engineers in the community to find out how they survived. You may find a mentor for life, or even a future job. Seek out internships or summer jobs in engineering. Your school and the national engineering organizations can help you find them. These opportunities may actually pay fairly well, help connect you to the real-world applications of your chosen field, and could very well lead to employment after graduation.

While not all internships are paid, a 2005 survey by the National Association of Colleges and Employers (NACE) found that nearly 98 percent of employers reported paying interns—and at an average of $15.44 an hour. Meanwhile, 95 percent reported they paid undergraduate co-op students, with average pay at $15.64 per hour. In addition, employers said that three out of five of their new college hires had internship experience while almost one-third had participated in a co-op assignment.

There are also campus activities outside of the engineering area. UConn's Allen says he and his fellow students were encouraged to branch out into other activities but "we weren't encouraged by the same people who gave us the work. You'd have the dean of engineering talking to us, telling us how hard the work is and (that) the average engineering student spends four and a half years getting a degree and then the kids in liberal arts were telling us, 'join as many clubs as you can.'"

It will be up to you to make the choice that's right for you. Remember, engineering is all about solving problems. If your engineering program turns out to be a "problem," you're fully capable of coming up with some creative ways to solve it. By doing so, you will be a better engineer in the real world.

What about Grades?

Will getting involved in activities outside the classroom affect your grades? Don't you need to have the very best grades possible?

Penn State's Wormley notes that "people develop at different stages of their career," and that while being in the top 10 to 15 percent of an engineering class means that a graduate is likely going to be a very good engineer, "when people have not been in the top 10 or 15 percent, they still have done exceptionally well."

"Many of our very successful alumni have come from a variety of places in their class, but they have been involved in a variety of activities outside of the classroom, such as professional societies and internships and they've shown leadership on campus," says Wormley. "Those things, coupled with a strong academic undergraduate program, lead to a lot of successes."

Allen says the engineering students on his campus take pride in their academic load. "We feel as if we get more work and we have to work harder," he says. "You can tell an engineer by the way we look, that we're more concentrated on our schoolwork than on the social activities that go on around class time."

The signs, he says, include torn jeans, "stuff in upper pockets, pencils sticking out everywhere, and we're usually unshaven."

For students who begin to struggle, there are lots of safety nets on every campus, from tutoring to study groups to working closely with your professors to find a way to succeed, but they can only help you if you seek them out. Don't be afraid to do that. Keep your focus on the end result and use your problem-solving skills to get you there.

How Long Will It Take?

Most schools offer four-year bachelor's degrees in engineering. Some offer five-year programs that end with a master's degree. Co-op programs, which combine classroom study with work in the field, generally last five or six years.

Once you get past the end of your sophomore year and have begun more concentrated study in a specific field, it is nearly impossible to move to another discipline without adding time to your college career.

"Pick what type of engineering you want very carefully," advises Allen, saying he has been surprised at how many engineering students decide they wish they had chosen another field "but they've gone so far, they've got to keep going. It's too late to change and still finish within four years."

Meanwhile, some in the engineering field wonder whether four years of coursework is sufficient training for such a technical profession. "There is a big argument ongoing in the engineering profession that's been going on for more than 50 years as to how much education should an engineer have before he leaves the halls of academia to begin practicing," says William C. Anderson, the executive director of the Council of Engineering and Scientific Specialty Boards (CESB).

Anderson notes that there have been efforts over time to increase the number of years of schooling required to five or six years, and that the American Society of Civil Engineers is now suggesting that five are necessary.

Meanwhile, a National Academy of Engineering report entitled "Educating the Engineer of 2020: Adapting Engineering Education to the New Century" recommends the engineering undergraduate degree be considered pre-engineering or an "engineering in training degree," with the master's degree recognized as the "professional degree."

"Between 1930 and now there has been a veritable technological explosion and at the same time, the amount of credit hours needed to obtain an engineering degree has been steadily reduced to 120 to 128 semester hours of credit," says Anderson, adding that when he graduated in the 1960s the requirement was 160 hours, which often required more than four years to complete.

Now, he says, some employers not only desire licensed Professional Engineers, which generally requires at least four years of work after college plus 16 hours of exams; some also prefer to hire engineers who are certified in very specific areas.

"I think some people understand the inadequacy of a standard engineering education, that it provides you with the basics but not much beyond that. Of course, that varies by school. Some are more focused on turning out engineers to practice in the real world, designing projects and all. Others see it as the beginning point in a long academic career focusing more on research."

In the end, it will be what you make of it. Plenty of people want you to succeed, not the least of whom are your parents, your teachers, and the institution of higher learning that said, "Come study engineering with us." It will be up to you to find your way.

"Doing well in engineering is 90 percent hard work and 10 percent intelligence," notes Allen. "I know kids who got 1100 on their SATs who are doing better than those who got 1400s. High school did not prepare me for engineering. First semester freshman year prepared me for engineering."

As you continue on your journey, also keep in mind Thomas Edison's advice that "genius is 1 percent inspiration and 99 percent perspiration." Be ready to perspire and have some fun along the way.

What Must Engineers Learn?

In order to obtain voluntary accreditation from ABET, the Accreditation Board for Engineering and Technology, engineering programs must show that their students will attain:

- An ability to apply knowledge of mathematics, science, and engineering
- An ability to design and conduct experiments, as well as to analyze and interpret data

- An ability to design a system, component, or process to meet desired needs within realistic constraints such as economic, environmental, social, political, ethical, health and safety, manufacturability, and sustainability
- An ability to function on multidisciplinary teams
- An ability to identify, formulate, and solve engineering problems
- An understanding of professional and ethical responsibility
- An ability to communicate effectively
- The broad education necessary to understand the impact of engineering solutions in a global, economic, environmental, and societal context
- A recognition of the need for, and an ability to engage in, lifelong learning
- A knowledge of contemporary issues
- An ability to use the techniques, skills, and modern engineering tools necessary for engineering practice

How students obtain those abilities is up to the institution within certain frameworks, as in requiring "one year of a combination of college level mathematics and basic sciences (some with experimental experience) appropriate to the discipline."

However, ABET becomes a bit more specific when it comes to disciplines. For example, this is what is required of a civil engineering program curriculum:

"The program must demonstrate that graduates have: proficiency in mathematics through differential equations, probability and statistics, calculus-based physics, and general chemistry; proficiency in a minimum of four (4) recognized major civil engineering areas; the ability to conduct laboratory experiments and to critically analyze and interpret data in more than one of the recognized major civil engineering areas; the ability to perform civil engineering design by means of design experiences integrated throughout the professional component of the curriculum; and an understanding of professional practice issues such as: procurement of work, bidding versus quality-based selection processes, how the design professionals and the construction professions interact to construct a project, the importance of professional licensure and continuing education, and/or other professional practice issues."

Building an Engineering School from the Ground Up

Just outside Boston, a new engineering school is providing an innovative undergraduate engineering education—tuition-free—that combines rigorous science and engineering fundamentals, entrepreneurship, and the liberal arts.

The Franklin W. Olin College of Engineering opened in the fall of 2002, thanks to one of the largest grants in the history of American higher education. It has approximately 300 academically exceptional undergraduates on its Needham, Massachusetts, campus.

The F.W. Olin Foundation decided to build the college to offer a new model for engineering education, including the National Science Foundation's recommendations for more emphasis on business and entrepreneurship, teamwork and communication.

Females comprise about 40 percent of the students and the faculty.

Olin prides itself on team-oriented projects and a real-world approach that culminates in the Senior Consulting Program for Engineering, where students take on a year-long engineering project for an actual client.

"We are heavily focused on combinations of technical knowledge, design, and social factors that are all necessary to engineering," says Dr. Sherra Kerns, Olin's vice president for Innovation and Research. "We look at things in terms of being able to realize products that meet needs."

The school offers majors in Electrical and Computer Engineering, Mechanical Engineering and "Engineering" as a general program of study that allows for individual options. Each student receives a four-year, full-tuition scholarship worth about $130,000.

CHAPTER 9

The Organized You for Fun and Profit

A mind-boggling array of support

If there is one trait that best defines an engineer it is the ability to concentrate on one subject to the complete exclusion of everything else in the environment. This sometimes causes engineers to be pronounced dead prematurely.

–Engineering blog

The number of professional societies connected to engineering—and their assorted abbreviations—is mind-boggling.

NSPE, ASEE, ASME, IEEE, AIChE, SWE, and so on. The alphabet soup combinations would make any engineering student's head spin.

In fact, there are so many groups that there is even an American Association of Engineering Societies that is, itself, comprised of 26 member societies.

Engineering groups seem to be everywhere—on college campuses, in high school classrooms, and out in the workplace. At Penn State alone, there are 50 organizations available to engineering students.

These groups can provide invaluable reinforcement and networking opportunities for students, but what if you're not, by nature, a joiner? Why should you care that there are so many opportunities out there for you to pay membership dues?

Again, the primary answer is: math and science.

Or, to be even clearer: technology.

As a potential engineer, you already know that technology isn't static. In fact, it's advancing more quickly than you can imagine even during the time it will take you to finish reading this book. So unless you have the time each day to research all of the pertinent developments in your field, or engineering in general, you'd better think about joining a society if you want to keep up.

It will make your job easier. In fact, it might even save it—or someone's life. Refined techniques are often introduced in peer group meetings. Professional journals often discuss new solutions that get around old hazards.

Whether you're studying engineering or already practicing it, you need to stay on top of the latest engineering developments. Even if you're still just thinking about engineering, several of these national societies have K–12 programs to help you learn more about the field as well.

What's in It for Me?

What can these professional organizations offer you? Continuing education. They may provide it informally through newsletters and magazines, and/or more formally via seminars and conventions.

"My feeling about professional engineering societies is that once you've graduated, they are the most efficient way to stay abreast of the changes in your field of engineering," says Bill Salmon, interim executive director of the American Association of Engineering Societies.

These groups also provide career development, networking, and job opportunities. They may be able to tell you how much money you should be making and where you can make it. They advocate for engineering and engineering issues in state legislatures and on Capitol Hill. In addition, they have codes of ethics they would like you to follow and standards of practice to keep your discipline as professional as possible.

Some sell books to help you, tools you need to do your job, and even clothing to proclaim your membership to the world.

There are groups that operate internationally, nationally, regionally, and/or on the local level. There are so many that surely one, or two, are right for you.

On campus, student engineering chapters and clubs provide valuable peer support. Many national groups provide awards and scholarships, sources of mentoring for you and opportunities for you to mentor younger students, as well as co-op and internship possibilities. They often provide speakers, tours, and hands-on opportunities to allow you to explore engineering further.

There are student groups organized for specific disciplines, certain grade point averages, just for women, and even for assorted ethnic backgrounds.

"They also provide an opportunity for students to be in touch with professionals in their field in their region and to become acquainted with what the society has to offer," explains Salmon. "They are a way to stay abreast of changes in your field, and act as an early introduction to how the society operates."

Many campuses also are home to engineering-related honor societies that invite top students to join their ranks. Tau Beta Pi (*www.tbp.org*) is the only one representing the entire engineering profession. Founded in 1885, it has chapters at 230 U.S. colleges and universities. Undergraduate students must be in the top eighth of their junior class or the top fifth of their senior class to receive invitations. Graduate students, alumni, and certain practicing engineers also may apply for membership. The group even offers an on-campus program to develop interpersonal skills to work in team and group settings.

There also are honor societies for the various disciplines, including Omega Chi Epsilon for chemical engineering (*www.che.utoledo.edu/oxe*), Chi Epsilon for civil engineering (*www.chi-epsilon.org*), Eta Kappa Nu for electrical and computer engineering (*www.hkn.org*), Alpha Pi Mu for industrial engineering (*www.alphapimu.net*), and Pi Tau Sigma (*www.pitausigma.net*) for mechanical engineering.

There is no doubt that joining a group related to your area of engineering interest can be invaluable after graduation.

"Once you're into your career after you've graduated, my feeling is that it's essential to be an active member of your engineering society. More and more, engineering is changing so rapidly that to remain at the front of your field, you've got to stay in touch with new developments," Salmon says.

He believes that societies also provide an avenue for engineers to contribute to their profession by sharing knowledge, particularly in the areas of research or new field testing efforts, with their community of colleagues through research papers and other avenues.

Steve Parkinson, a 1975 graduate of Northeastern University who now heads the Public Works Department in Portsmouth, New Hampshire, agrees.

"They keep you up on the latest technology and give you an opportunity for meeting with your peers and your equivalents. It allows you to compare what you're doing with what they're doing. It's almost a verification of knowledge," he says.

Crossing Disciplines

Societies also can provide expertise and support that cross discipline lines.

Jamiyo Mack, an African-American female chemical engineer now working for a major consulting firm in suburban Washington, DC, says she has belonged to more than one group because "each one has their own focus," offering her different levels of support along with the opportunity to keep up on new developments and make contacts.

"With the Society of Women Engineers, you have the camaraderie of women, even if you may be of a different race. With the National Society of Black Engineers, it helps you remember that while you may be the only black in your job, you're not the only one out there," she says.

In addition, some engineering and engineering-related organizations offer voluntary certification in technical specialties. For example, the American Academy of Environmental Engineers (AAEE) offers Diplomate Environmental Engineer certifications in Air Pollution Control; Hazardous Waste Management; Industrial Hygiene; Radiation Protection; Solid Waste Management, and Water Supply and Wastewater.

Alternatively, certification may be offered in a subject that spans disciplines. The American Society of Mechanical Engineers, American Society of Civil Engineers, American Institute of Chemical Engineers, and American Institute of Mining, Metallurgical, and Petroleum Engineers combined forces to offer fundamental and professional level certifications in engineering management.

Certification generally requires a certain amount of engineering experience after graduation and before a candidate can even apply for the designation, as well as an oral or written exam, and continuing professional development.

Certification application fees range from about $50 to $150, with exam fees adding another $100 to $200. There also is an annual fee of $75 to $150 to maintain certification, plus the cost of any required continuing education.

"Societies offer certification as a way to enable individual engineers to demonstrate by way of some form of an examination, or a review of their work history by a peer panel and other credentials, that they are competent in a specialty area of engineering, or an engineering-related science," explains William C. Anderson, executive director of the Council of Engineering and Scientific Specialty Boards (CESB), which accredits engineering certification programs. "It improves their hiring potential in the marketplace.

"Another reason for certification is a move by the profession to provide a way to keep the bad guys out, the people who are not competent, from practicing in that specialty."

Currently, there is really no national oversight of the engineering profession. States license engineers and their requirements vary. Only about 20 to 25 percent of the practicing engineers are licensed Professional Engineers, which requires verification of a certain level of knowledge.

So it is not surprising, Anderson says, that "engineering, in general, is a profession where practitioners are generally credential-adverse," unlike other professions such as medicine where credentials are highly regarded.

Even if obtaining credentials is not in your future, professional organizations can provide what you need to keep you just that—professional—in the workplace and help you get to the workplace if you're still a student.

Who's Who

Here is a sampling of the types of engineering societies out there that have campus chapters. Some also have activities and information for younger students, or ways for their membership to provide outreach to children in grades K–12:

- **American Institute of Chemical Engineers,** *www.AIChE.org*
  - Over 40,000 members worldwide
  - 18 divisions and forums, and six technical societies
  - 150 campus chapters, some of which compete to build a chemically powered vehicle
  - Offers scholarships
  - National student membership is $15
  - Some pre-university resources
- **The American Society of Civil Engineers,** *www.asce.org*
  - Claims more than 133,000 members
  - 400 local affiliates
  - Four younger member councils, 230 student chapters, 36 student clubs, and six international student groups
  - Founded in 1852
  - Offers competitions like the National Steel Bridge Competition and the National Concrete Canoe Competition
  - Offers scholarships
  - Student membership is free
  - Has K–12 resources
- **American Society for Engineering Education,** *www.asee.org*
  - Claims more than 12,000 deans, professors, instructors, students and industry representatives
  - Eight campus chapters

- Nonprofit member association founded in 1893, "dedicated to promoting and improving engineering and engineering technology education"
- Hosts the *www.k12engineering.org* Web site as part of its outreach efforts
- Offers scholarships
- Student membership is $20
- **American Society of Mechanical Engineers,** *www.asme.org*
  - Founded in 1880
  - 120,000 members and 37 technical divisions
  - 400 student sections worldwide
  - Student competitions include building human-powered vehicles that may be for use on land, in water, or the air
  - Offers scholarships
  - Free limited national membership during first year of college, $25 annually until graduation
  - Pre-college resources
- **Engineers Without Borders-USA,** *www.ewb-usa.com*
  - Approximately 3,000 members
  - 32 professional chapters and 100 campus chapters
  - Nonprofit humanitarian organization established in 2000 to partner with developing communities worldwide in order to improve their quality of life
  - Partnership involves implementation of sustainable engineering projects, while involving and training internationally responsible engineers and engineering students
  - Offers scholarships
  - $15 student membership fee
  - Not affiliated with Doctors Without Borders
- **Institute of Electrical and Electronics Engineers, Inc.,** *www.ieee.org*
  - More than 365,000 members worldwide
  - 39 societies and five technical councils
  - More than 1,300 student branches across the globe
  - Computer design competition
  - Offers scholarships

- Student membership costs $30
- Pre-university resources
- **Institute of Industrial Engineers,** *www.iienet.org*
  - Over 15,000 members
  - 280 chapters worldwide (including 180 student chapters), with 20 technical divisions and three societies
  - Founded in 1948 to support the industrial engineering profession and individuals involved with improving quality and productivity
  - Members include undergraduate and graduate students, engineering practitioners and consultants in all industries, engineering managers, and engineers in education, research, and government
  - Student scholarships available
  - Student membership costs $30
  - Pre-university resources
- **Society of Women Engineers,** *www.swe.org*
  - Approximately 18,000 members
  - Nearly 100 professional sections, 300 student sections, and members-at-large in all engineering and technology disciplines
  - K–12 outreach programs
  - Founded in 1950
  - Not-for-profit educational and service organization
  - Scholarships offered
  - New student membership is $20
- **National Society of Professional Engineers,** *www.nspe.org*
  - 50,000 members in 53 state and territorial societies
  - More than 500 chapters
  - Founded in 1934 to be the recognized voice and advocate of licensed Professional Engineers
  - In 1951, launched National Engineers Week and, "by partnering with other societies and industry, has built it into the most popular annual celebration of engineering in the country"
  - Scholarships offered
  - $20 student dues, except $45 in California and $60 in Virginia
  - Pre-university resources

Here is a list of some other well-known engineering and engineering-related organizations (some of which have non-engineer members) and their Web sites by practice areas:

- **Agricultural**—American Society of Agricultural and Biological Engineers, *www.asabe.org*, campus branches, scholarships
- **Aerospace**—American Institute of Aeronautics and Astronautics, Inc., *www.aiaa.org*, campus branches, scholarships, pre-university resources
- **Biomedical**—Biomedical Engineering Society, *www.bmes.org*, campus chapters, scholarships; Institute of Biological Engineering, *www.ibeweb.org*, campus chapters, academic program list
- **Chemical**—American Institute of Chemical Engineers, *www.AIChE.org* (information about this group described earlier); American Chemical Society, *www.chemistry.org*, campus chapters, scholarships, K–12 resources
- **Civil**—American Society of Civil Engineers, *www.asce.org* (information about this group described earlier); Structural Engineering Institute, *www.seinstitute.org*
- **Computer hardware**—IEEE Computer Society, *www.computer.org* (for info on IEEE, see earlier description), campus chapters, scholarships, pre-university resources
- **Electrical and electronics**—Institute of Electrical and Electronics Engineers–USA, *www.ieeeusa.org* (part of **Institute of Electrical and Electronics Engineers, Inc.,** *www.ieee.org* (see earlier description); The Illuminating Engineering Society of North America, *www.iesna.org*, nonengineer members, student chapters, limited K–12 resources
- **Environmental**—American Academy of Environmental Engineers, *www.aaee.net*, some career information
- **Health and safety**—American Society of Safety Engineers, *www.asse.org*, campus chapters, scholarships, career information, not all members are engineers; Society of Fire Protection Engineers, *www.sfpe.org*, campus chapters, pre-university resources
- **Industrial**—Institute of Industrial Engineers, *www.iienet.org* (see earlier description)

- **Materials**—The Minerals, Metals, & Materials Society, *www.tms.org*, campus chapters, scholarships, pre-university resources; ASM International (The Materials Information Society), *www.asminternational.org*, campus chapters, scholarships, K–12 outreach
- **Mechanical**—American Society of Mechanical Engineers, *www.asme.org* (see earlier description); American Society of Heating, Refrigerating, and Air-Conditioning Engineers, Inc., *www.ashrae.org*, campus chapters, scholarships, K–12 resources; Society of Automotive Engineers, *www.sae.org*, campus chapters, scholarships, K–12 resources
- **Marine engineers and naval architects**—Society of Naval Architects and Marine Engineers, *www.sname.org*, student sections, scholarships, pre-university resources
- **Mining and geological, including mining safety**—The Society for Mining, Metallurgy, and Exploration, Inc., *www.smenet.org*, campus chapters, scholarships, K–12 information at Mineral Information Institute, *www.mii.org*
- **Nuclear**—American Nuclear Society, *www.ans.org*, campus chapters, scholarships, pre-university resources
- **Petroleum**—Society of Petroleum Engineers, *www.spe.org*, campus chapters, scholarships, K–12 resources

Here are some examples of minority engineering groups (for more information, see Chapter 5):

- **American Indian Science and Engineering Society (AISES),** *www.aises.org*, campus chapters, scholarships, limited K–12 resources
- **Chinese Institute of Engineers (CIE/USA),** *www.cie-usa.org*, promotes Chinese-American Engineers/Scientists and their fellow Asian-Americans
- **National Action Council for Minorities in Engineering (NACME),** *www.nacme.org*, campus chapters, scholarships, K–12 resources
- **National Society of Black Engineers (NSBE),** *www.nsbe.org*, campus chapters, scholarships, pre-college initiative grades 6–12

- **Society of Hispanic Professional Engineers (SHPE),** *www.shpe.org*, campus chapters, scholarships, limited K–12 resources
- **Women in Engineering Programs & Advocates Network (WEPAN),** *www.wepan.org*, campus chapters, scholarships, K–12 resources

CHAPTER 10

Transition

Looking forward, looking back

"I've heard of students being asked, 'What are your weaknesses?' Don't tell him what your weaknesses are."
—Tom Tarantelli, Director of the Career Development
Center at Rensselaer Polytechnic Institute

T here are thousands of ways young people find their way into engineering careers, and the stories of Carlisle Daniel and Toby Keller are just two of them. Like most paths to the same destination, they are each unique in some ways and yet also have strong similarities.

At the time we talked to them, Daniel was a year and half away from graduating from Virginia Tech in Blacksburg, Virginia, and Keller was in his first year with Boeing in Seattle.

Looking Forward

Carlisle Daniel says he has no idea how long he's been interested in engineering, but thinks it started pretty early.

"Probably since I was two; I was taking things apart all the time," he says. "I think I've always liked working with my hands. Things in liberal arts just never had much appeal to me."

Carlisle credits his father, Harrison, as having put him on the road to an engineering career. The older Daniel has a PhD in engineering and is a mining engineer with the government, having done consulting work as far away as Poland.

For Carlisle, however, engines have always been a passion, pushing him in the direction of mechanical engineering. "I'd love to do something with cars (after college), or racing trucks—maybe in the aftermarket."

Like many other engineering students, Daniel found himself drawn to math and science classes in high school, where he excelled. "I was pretty good in calculus and (advanced placement) chemistry. They were really never much of a problem to me."

One of his chief regrets, however, was never taking any computer programming classes.

"I had some problems my freshman year because I had no idea how to do computer programming. My second year here I took a class, but I was way behind and even now I have problems with the basics. If I had it to do over again, I've have taken programming in high school."

Otherwise, at Virginia Tech, he admits to being bored with some classes his first and second year. "The liberal arts classes and electives weren't that interesting. And at the time, I actually thought the math, physics, and chemistry classes were pretty pointless—until I started taking the upper-level (engineering) classes and it all started fitting together."

Daniel admits that engineers have—and maybe deserve—reputations as being hardworking students with limited social skills—in other words, nerds.

"Yeah, there are some of those here, but it's the kind of thing you bring upon yourself," he says. "So many people drop out (of engineering school) because the work is so hard and it's no fun. Especially in the first and second years, they're doing classwork every night while all the other guys in the dorm are going out and having a good time. That makes it hard."

Daniel managed to avoid that feeling of deprivation by studying between classes during the day. "I was always able to hang out with my friends at night if I wanted to. It's really a time management thing."

One of the best things about Virginia Tech, he says, is that students have an opportunity to work on projects even in the first year. Student projects have included designing and building remote-controlled airplanes, remote-controlled cars, and human-powered submarines. Some classes have developed cars propelled by fuel cells rather than gasoline and another group built a miniature Formula One race car.

Daniel says he was involved in designing, building, and racing a miniature Baja car—a tube-framed car with a small 10-horsepower engine that competed across rugged terrain against cars produced at other colleges.

As he faced his final year in school, Daniel was uncertain what the future would bring. The previous summer he had worked as an intern and learned a great deal. "A lot of it was actually applying some of the things I learned at school."

He found the internship through a career fair held on the campus, but didn't hold out much hope that future career fairs would lead to full employment.

"The career fairs here mostly attract Virginia companies or East Coast companies. What I'd really like to do eventually is get a job back home [in Colorado]. I'm not really sure how I'm going to do that. I'll have to figure something out."

Looking Back

For Toby Keller, a first-year engineer at Boeing, perseverance—and maybe a bit of luck—paid off in the job he'd always wanted.

During his final years at the University of New Hampshire's School of Engineering, Keller found the Boeing Web site and shortly thereafter discovered that the company offered paid internships.

"I kept checking the Web site and they kept posting different internships, so I just kept applying." Unfortunately, none of them panned out. "So when I reached my senior year, I stopped applying for internships and started applying for jobs. I used all the same information about myself; I just changed 'intern' for 'employment.'

"Then I checked my e-mail one day and there was a message from Boeing inviting me out to Seattle for a collegiate job fair. They were inviting a lot of graduating engineers from around the country out to the headquarters. I interviewed and it went really well. It was pretty obvious to me that's where I wanted to work and, I guess, it was pretty obvious to them, too."

Because he essentially had a job by the middle of his senior year, Keller did not participate in on-campus job fairs, nor did he ever apply to smaller companies.

"I don't think I would have been comfortable in a smaller company," he said.

Far from leaving his classroom days behind, as soon as Keller arrived at Boeing he began his education all over again. After being assigned to a department, "the first thing you do is start training. You do that for the first few weeks you're there."

After that, he was assigned to a team involved with aircraft design and construction.

"The team was made up of people in various age ranges. I was the youngest and there was a guy on the team who had come out of training just a few weeks before me. But there were also people in their 50s who had been with the company for years."

In the beginning, Keller said his team was involved in planning and processes. "The best part was that we'd actually go out on the plant floor and talk to the people working on the planes. Those guys probably taught me as much as anyone else did."

After several weeks on a team, members rotate to other teams and new people are brought in. "That way you get to learn the whole company," Keller said.

Keller's hope was to move into aerospace design for Boeing. Before then, he also hoped to re-enroll in college to get a master's degree.

"Eventually, I'd like to work with NASA," he said. "We'll see."

Let Your School Help

Tom Tarantelli, director of the Career Development Center at Rensselaer Polytechnic, suggests that the entire college experience is one of looking for a career—it's not just something that occurs in the senior year.

"It actually begins before you set foot on a campus," he says. "Looking for a career begins when you are deciding what school you want to go to and what you want your major to be. It's about fulfilling goals and ambitions, finding your passion."

He acknowledges that "it's one of life's cruel fates" that high school students are asked to start setting their career paths before they are really mature enough to make that kind of decision. At Rensselaer, career development begins at freshman orientation and carries on through graduation. Beginning their first year, students receive opportunities to interact with the school's alumni—to talk with them about the choices they made during school and the opportunities they've had since leaving.

"What we're really teaching them from the beginning is the power of networking. Make conversation," Tarantelli says.

In classes, students learn the technical aspects of employment; at the Career Center, they learn the human aspects of finding employment. Like most colleges, Rensselaer offers career fairs where invited corporations come to the campus and talk with students about job openings. The Career Center urges students to take advantage of those fairs.

Like other schools, Rensselaer also invites specific corporations to come to the campus where they can meet with students in more private settings. The Career Center sponsors a series of dinners on campus (see page 127) where as many as 60 students at a time may sit down with potential employers in a more casual setting.

Beyond those formal job placement opportunities, however, Tarantelli says students join professional societies on campus that assist in finding jobs after graduation, and students also are encouraged to come to the Career Center "Café" where they can browse online data about thousands of companies worldwide. (Some campuses call these centers *resource rooms*.)

Tarantelli says students are encouraged to apply for summer internships. "You'd be amazed at the number of students who return from those internships with full-time employment offers."

Co-ops also are a good route to a career choice. "Students will go and work for eight or nine months with a company and then come back here to finish up their degrees. Many of those also result in job offers."

Like Toby Keller and Boeing, the Career Center also urges students to go onto specific corporate Web sites and see what various companies have to offer. Says Tarantelli, "You want to know as much about a company as possible before you apply."

Rensselaer recently surveyed its alumni to ask how they ended up where they were. The study found:

1. 29 percent accepted a full-time employment offer as a result of a summer internship secured through the Career Center
2. 21 percent found employment through a friend or relative
3. 10 percent found employment through the Career Center
4. 6 percent found employment with the help of a faculty member
5. 5½ percent found employment through online sources

"What we found was that about 60 percent of our graduates had jobs waiting for them after graduation, another 2 or 3 percent were involved in ROTC and went into the military, and about 20 percent went on to graduate school."

Tarantelli's Career Center also offers help to the students in a variety of other ways. "We have group discussions on how to do interviews, and how to write a resume. We talk about how to communicate with corporate executives, and even how to write e-mails and follow-up letters."

Also discussed are how to dress, proper behavior, and other aspects of the interview process. The school even has video rehearsals where students can watch themselves in mock interview situations and critique their performances.

"We even teach them how to do an 'elevator speech' or '60-second sell,'" when a student only has a very short period to impress a potential employer.

How to Have Dinner

One of the many things Rensselaer engineering students review in their preparation for employment is what to do when the recruiter or company executive invites them to dinner.

First, says Tom Tarantelli of the school's Career Center, don't kid yourself into thinking that this is a social event. "Dinner is part of the interview," Tarantelli says. "The company wants to see how you are in a social setting."

Here are some tips:

- Before you get there: "Dress appropriately for the restaurant. Turn off your cell phone."
- Where to sit: "When you walk in, take your lead from the employer. Let him or her point out where you should sit. Don't take your seat until the employer takes his seat."
- First thing: "Take your napkin and place it on your lap."
- Beverage: "Never order alcohol. Ice tea is safe, or water."
- What to order: "Something in middle range of the menu. Don't order the most expensive thing. More importantly, don't order something with a heavy sauce or soup—no spaghetti or linguini. Don't order anything messy" that could get on your clothes.
- During dinner: "Take small bites. There is nothing worse that having taken a big mouthful of food and suddenly having the recruiter ask you a question. If you take small bites you can swallow and answer the question."
- What to discuss: "This is an opportunity for the employer to see who you really are. He already knows your grade point average. He knows your technical skills. If the employer is an alumnus of your school, make sure you're up-to-date on what's happening on campus. Read the school newspaper."

In general, says Tarantelli, there are several questions that you should be careful in answering.

The first one is when the recruiter says, "Tell me about yourself." For some reason this stumps a lot of students. "He wants to know about your interests and what you've done. Try to relate your personal experiences. This is your chance to show that you're unique. Be positive."

That also goes for another dreaded question.

"I've heard of students being asked, 'What are your weaknesses?' Don't tell him what your weaknesses are. Again, relate a negative experience but how you turned it into a positive experience, or how you overcame it or worked through it. Again, the idea is to be positive."

The worst question he ever heard a student asked: "What's your favorite color?"

"But again, say something like, 'Red, because it reminds me of a well-tuned sports car that I worked on.' Again, the idea is to relate your response to an experience with a positive ending."

CHAPTER 11

Can You Get a Job in This Business?

You bet—and the money ain't bad, either

"Engineering students have the lowest grade point averages, but the highest starting salaries."

–Campus lore

Not only are there lots of engineering jobs out there, but starting salaries are significantly higher than for other college majors—as much as one and a half to two times more.

And although the number of available jobs varies by specialty, the overall employment outlook for engineers is extremely positive.

Yes, there are nagging concerns about foreign outsourcing of more U.S. engineering jobs in a global economy, which is a trend that is of some concern (see Chapter 13). However, all indicators point to a continuing need for engineers right here in the United States—and to employers willing to pay well for their expertise.

"The prospects are fantastic for engineers," proclaims Kathryn Gray, president of the National Society of Professional Engineers. "There are so many job opportunities and one reason is that we have an inordinate number of Professional Engineers approaching retirement but there are not as many engineers coming into the system as we have retiring.

"Another issue we are dealing with is the number of students who consider engineering when they enter college and, after receiving the basic degree, choose to do something different.

"That leaves us with all of the initiatives and all the projects that require engineers, and not enough entering the pipeline," says Gray, a civil engineer who started an engineering software firm in Illinois.

Even the U.S.-based staffing firm Manpower is among those reporting a talent shortage of qualified engineers across North America and Asia. Expect the positive employment situation for engineers to continue well into the future. Even now, the unemployment rate for engineers is far below the national average for all other occupations, with very few exceptions—and the average salary is far above it.

The NSPE has been conducting salary surveys for 50 years and each year, there is a consistent increase in wages for engineers, both at the entry level and among those with more experience. In 2005, the average salary for engineers from all disciplines with less than one year of experience was $46,059. With one to two years of experience, the average was $48,451.

The National Association of Colleges and Employers (NACE) also tracks salary offers for new college graduates, and engineers consistently rank at the top. The average salary offer for a 2006 chemical engineering graduate was $55,900, up 4.2 percent, for example.

Electrical engineering graduates received average offers of $52,899 and mechanical engineering graduates saw average offers of $50,672, according to NACE. Civil engineering graduates received average offers of $44,999. Granted, factors such as geography and licensing can affect the numbers. For example, new licensed engineers made an average salary of $51,383 in 2005.

Other NSPE statistics of interest:

- Nuclear engineers had the highest average annual salary of all disciplines at $119,643, followed by petroleum engineers at $117,004, in 2005.

- The average salary of executive-level engineers was $129,724.
- At an average $87,421, engineers in the Pacific Southwest states of California, Nevada, and Hawaii and engineers in the South Central region of Texas, Oklahoma, Arkansas, and Louisiana, who earned an average $85,470, made more than engineers in other regions.

The U.S. Bureau of Labor Statistics expects overall engineering employment to grow by 9 to 17 percent through the year 2014. (For projections by disciplines, see Table 11.2 or Chapter 3.)

The government anticipates the number of engineering graduates will roughly equal the number of job openings through 2014. While a smaller proportion of engineers leave their jobs each year compared to other professions, engineering is such a large profession that there always will be a need to replace those who transfer to management, retire, or leave the workforce.

Also important is the fact that many engineers work at jobs that are unaffected by economic slowdowns, such as long-term research and development projects.

However, there have been prior layoffs in the aerospace and electronics industries following major cutbacks in defense spending or in government-backed research and development. Some companies also have begun contracting with engineering service firms rather than hire engineers in-house. Table 11.1 summarizes the unemployment rates among engineering disciplines for 2005.

Employment Trends by Discipline

Mining engineers currently have by far the highest engineering unemployment rate and the number of their jobs is expected to decline through 2014, and likewise for jobs in petroleum engineering, because most U.S. mines and petroleum deposit areas are already developed. However, favorable opportunities are anticipated worldwide for U.S.-trained engineers in these fields.

Chemical engineers also have a relatively high unemployment rate compared to the other engineering disciplines. A contribut-

Table 11.1   Engineering Unemployment by Discipline in 2005

Discipline	Unemployment Rate
Aerospace	1.6%
Agricultural	--
Biomedical	--
Chemical	5.2%
Civil	0.3%
Computer hardware	1.4%
Electrical/electronics	1.7%
Environmental	1.5%
Industrial	2.3%
Marine	--
Materials	1.1%
Mechanical	2.6%
Mining and geological	18.9%
Nuclear	--
Petroleum	1.3%
Engineers, all other	0.7%
National	4.7%
Source: U.S. Department of Labor	

ing factor may be the fact that chemical companies closed 70 facilities and scheduled 40 more for shutdown in the United States in 2004, alone. In addition, no new refineries have been built in the United States since 1976. Of the 120 chemical plants under construction worldwide with $1 billion or higher price tags, only one is in the United States but 50 are in China.

Expect the biomedical and environmental engineering disciplines to see the strongest job growth through 2014. The U.S. Government's Bureau of Labor Statistics believes technology will be a major factor in engineering job growth in America, as well as in an engineer's personal job growth.

Table 11.2 summarizes projected job growth by engineering discipline through the year 2014.

Stay Productive and Stay Educated

Employers continue to rely on engineers to increase the productivity of their companies, and improve and update product designs under pressure from competition and the rapid changes in technology. While the government expects technological advances to limit future job opportunities in many professions, this definitely will not be true in engineering because technology will lead to the development of new products and processes.

The U.S. government also is among those that believe it is essential for engineers "to continue their education throughout their careers because much of their value to their employer depends on their knowledge of the latest technology." Those who do not, particularly engineers working in high-technology areas, risk layoffs or being passed over for promotions.

In addition, engineers who want to retain their Professional Engineer licenses must continue their professional education as a requirement for licensing renewal in many states.

Where Do Engineers Actually Work?

The good news for you is that engineers are employed everywhere, both in terms of types of workplace and geography. More than one-third of the engineering jobs in the United States are in manufacturing, but every industry employs engineers. The federal, state, and local governments also employ a good number. There are engineering jobs in large cities and in rural areas, and every place in between.

Table 11.2 Engineering Job Growth Projections by Discipline through 2014

Occupation	Total employment (in 1,000s)		2004–2014 change in total employment		2004–2014 average annual job openings (in 1,000s)		2004 Median annual earnings (Dollars)
	2004	2014	Number (1,000s)	Percent	Due to growth and total replacement needs	Due to growth and net replacement needs	
Total, all occupations	145,612	164,540	18,928	13	26,090	5,468	--
Aerospace engineers	76	82	6	8.3	6	2	79,100
Agricultural engineers	3	4	--	12	--	--	56,520
Biomedical engineers	10	13	3	30.7	1	--	67,690
Chemical engineers	31	34	3	10.6	3	1	76,770
Civil engineers	237	276	39	16.5	19	8	64,230
Computer hardware engineers	77	84	8	10.1	5	2	81,150
Electrical engineers	156	174	18	11.8	12	5	71,610
Electronics engineers, except computer	143	157	14	9.7	11	4	75,770
Environmental engineers	49	64	15	30	5	2	66,480

Health and safety engineers, except mining safety engineers and inspectors	27	30	4	13.4	2	1	63,730
Industrial engineers	177	205	28	16	13	7	65,020
Marine engineers and naval architects	7	7	1	8.5	--	--	72,040
Materials engineers	21	24	3	12.2	2	1	67,110
Mechanical engineers	226	251	25	11.1	11	9	66,320
Mining and geological engineers, including mining safety engineers	5	5	--	-1.5	--	--	64,690
Nuclear engineers	17	19	1	7.3	1	1	84,880
Petroleum engineers	16	16	--	-0.1	1	1	88,500
Engineers, all others	172	198	27	15.4	19	6	74,430
Engineering, managers	190	215	25	13	15	6	97,630

Source: U.S. Department of Labor Bureau of Labor Statistics

For the most part, you could find a job in your discipline almost anywhere. The exceptions would be disciplines that may be concentrated in certain geographic areas, such as ocean and marine engineering—or petroleum engineering jobs in areas of large deposits.

The majority of engineers physically work in office buildings, industrial plants, or labs and most do so during a 40-hour work-week. There are some disciplines, however, where engineers work on job sites or travel extensively between sites and their offices.

Experienced engineers who seek more independence and flexibility than in a standard engineering job may pursue consulting or contract engineering. The downside is a higher degree of financial insecurity.

How Will You Find a Job After Graduation?

Fortunately for you, engineers continue to be in high demand. Your college or university offers some degree of career placement guidance and opportunities, as it does for all its majors, but you should not hesitate to ask now how many engineering graduates find jobs immediately after graduation.

Some schools hold engineering job fairs that provide an opportunity to meet with many large firms seeking engineers.

The professional societies and organizations listed in Chapter 9 also have valuable employment resources. Some even help you write your resume and provide important job-hunting tips. All have some sort of employment center for their members, such as job boards or updated salary information. In addition, these organizations provide opportunities for networking and the continuing education you will find so necessary to keep up with your exciting and fast-moving profession once you're on the job.

In addition to the engineering associations, there are other groups that sell in-depth salary information updated annually, including the Engineering Workforce Commission (*www.ewc-online.org*) and NACE (*www.naceweb.org*). Large online employment sites, such as *www.monster.com*, also have engineering salary information available.

Getting Started

Big or small, what's it going to be?

"There are three principal ways to lose money: wine, women, and engineers. While the first two are more pleasant, the third is by far the more certain."
          –Baron Rothschild, ca. 1800

Congratulations on graduating. Now what?

Today's engineering student never had it so good. For the most part there are jobs out there in the world, starting salaries are really good, and there seem to be a lot of directions to choose from.

The first question is: Big firm or small? The answer is (as you might have already guessed): Well, it's pretty much up to you.

Even Ed Richardson, manager of engineering at Bechtel Corporation (and it's hard to get much bigger than Bechtel), says there are a lot of pros and cons, and which way to go really depends more on the interests of the engineer than the size of the company.

"If you go to work for a small company, you are going to do a lot of things early in your career," he says. "You're going to cover a lot more territory a lot faster than someone who joins a company the size of ours.

"You're going to get into estimating, you're going to get involved in design, you're going to be interacting with the customers a lot more, a lot sooner in your career."

And the downsides?

"You're going to be working on a lot of small projects. You're going to be working on shopping center upgrades and things like that.

"At a large company, you may be on a team of 50 to 500 other engineers. And projects you're working on are going to be a lot more challenging. One of the things we're doing right now is building an offshore airport at Qatar. It's a $5 billion airport and we're going to move 30 million cubic meters of seabed to use as fill to get it done. How many people get to work on something like that?

"In a large company, you can work on projects that change the world."

Still, he says, large firms are not a good choice for everyone.

"Again, in a smaller company you are getting a lot of experience in a lot of different things. You're going to be in charge of things quicker. You are going to take on more responsibility earlier."

A coin flip (good or bad) is the amount of travel you might be able (or forced) to do depending on the size of company you choose. With a smaller company, you're likely to become very familiar with your geographic territory. With a large company, you're more likely to see more of the world and probably get a chance to live overseas.

"In a company like ours, we work with engineers on their career path. We understand that if you aren't being challenged in the first five years, you won't stay."

The job-seeking college senior should note, however, that not all large companies are created equal. While firms like Bechtel move new civil engineers onto projects immediately, other kinds of engineers, such as manufacturing engineers, may see assignment to a specific product line and work there for years.

You could be assigned to a team that builds heat exchangers and never even move to a different building—let alone a different country.

Start Small and Grow Big

Joel Moskowitz, the founder of Ceradyne Corp., sees both sides of the big/small argument because he started his company with next to no capital some 40 years ago and has grown it into a nearly half-billion-dollar business—recently named the fastest-growing technology company in the United States.

"I started this company with $5,000, sitting at my kitchen table," he says today.

While in the Army in the early '60s, Moskowitz worked on ceramics on Nike Missiles. In 1963, however, he left the service and moved from New York to California to launch his own business.

"I went to night school at USC to earn an MBA," he said. His first contract for a ceramic missile component came from the Air Force for $25,000. From there, the company kept growing.

Moskowitz has a slightly different viewpoint from Richardson on the question of big company or small company.

"In big companies like General Electric, for two years you work in a division for six months and then they move you to something else. It's a good way to get to know the company before you decide what you want to do most.

"But in a small company, there is nothing that makes you want to move up the food chain faster than knowing that your product is what's paying the bills. If you're not making it and selling it, you're going to be out of business pretty quick. I think that aspect of a small company is terrific. There's a lot of pressure on you and you may not get to do a lot of different things, but you learn a lot about business.

"If you have a reasonable probability of success, [a small company] is the best thing that could ever happen. But for awhile it's going to be a struggle to make the payroll. And in some small companies, family members could dominate the top of the company. That can be an issue.

"For big companies, though, you're going to have a training program. That can be important."

Individual Choice

Gregory Bovid of Ayres & Associates in Midland, Michigan, believes the question of big firm/small firm is a strictly individual choice.

"If you don't like working in a big city, there are lots of jobs available in smaller environments," he says. "But, of course, it also depends a lot on what you want to do. Some time ago we hired a new engineer who wanted to work on water resource management. We put her on a project, but quite frankly we only get so many of those jobs. This week might be water resources; next week might be a highway design. She left and went to a larger firm where she does a lot of water projects."

Small Startup

Michael Lutz of Telemics, a six-person shop based in Louisville, Kentucky, sings the praises of small startup companies as the best route for any engineer.

"There are no clock punchers in a small startup," he says. "Everyone is focused as if the current project is a life or death situation for the company, because it usually is a life or death situation for the company."

Currently Telemics is rolling out a network that allows major cities such as Los Angeles to know when street lights are burning out. The company has developed a small component that is installed on each light and networked to a Web site. City workers can routinely go on the site and tell which lights are having problems.

"What's good about small startups is that everyone participates in the innovative process. Small companies that have been around for awhile sometimes act a lot like midsized companies. The owner has a way he likes to do things. He expects everyone to approach problems the same way. You don't have that problem in startups."

What about Government?

Another good source of employment for the starting engineer is in the government.

"It's a different atmosphere, private versus public," says Steve Parkinson, the Public Works director for the City of Portsmouth, New Hampshire.

"You have more security in a government situation than in a private enterprise. When the jobs don't come your way in the private world, you have to let staff go."

For those who are interested in public service, the U.S. government employs tens of thousands of engineers in hundreds of different roles, doing everything from supervising repairs on national monuments in Washington to helping build vehicles that will traverse the surface of Mars.

Moreover, what's good about working for the federal government is that the starting salaries tend to be pretty good, mentoring or some kind of training is typically provided, and the jobs can be located anywhere from the most isolated regions of Alaska to the urban settings of New York.

If you're interested in a good overview of what's out there, you can go to *www.USAjobs.gov*, type in the word "engineer" in the search engine and on any given day you may find 700 to 1,000 job opportunities. If you're a little more discriminating, however, all the U.S. government agencies have their own Web sites and all have employment sections.

There are a couple of obvious choices for engineers, such as NASA and the Army Corps of Engineers.

The Army Corps of Engineers, for example (*www.usace.army.mil/*), does extensive work in waterway navigation, flood control, environmental protection, and disaster response. It also designs and manages construction of military facilities for the Army and Air Force.

NASA (in addition to astronauts) always is in need of scientists and engineers in a wide variety of disciplines. The agency has a very active program of internships, cooperative programs, and summer employment. In the engineering realm, NASA needs electrical, mechanical, and civil engineers, but don't be afraid to apply even if your interests lie in microbiology or geology.

Military experience is often an advantage, but not required. The best place to start is at *www.NASAjobs.nasa.gov.*

The Nonprofit Sector

Nonprofits are doing some of the most important engineering work on the planet. An excellent example is Inveneo (*www.Inveneo.org*), a nonprofit based in San Francisco that is literally trying to connect the world to the Internet.

Inveneo works with third-world countries and in the remotest parts of developing nations to bring Internet and telephone communications to even the smallest, most isolated of villages where electrical power is sketchy and phone lines are nonexistent.

The company has developed a stationary bicycle that, when pedaled, charges a small battery that, in turn, powers a small computer that the company also developed. About 15 minutes of pedaling can provide about an hour's worth of computer time—time enough for someone to make contact with the outside world via VoIP/IP (voice over Internet protocols). A solar-powered version also is available.

To make sure the calls get to the outside world, Inveneo sets up Wi-Fi relay stations in remote jungles, desert oases, or anywhere else. The technology is relatively simple, relatively inexpensive, and typically can be set up in a matter of days—meaning it also can be rushed to disaster locations where power plants and communications have been destroyed.

Also on the nonprofit front, an organization called Engineers Without Borders (*www.ewb-usa.org*) has adopted the helpless and the hopeless as its primary cause. EWB does things like build schools and libraries in remote parts of the world. It brings fresh water to villages in Rwanda and electricity to Tajikistan in central Asia. Invariably, EWB volunteers function in areas without adequate security, medicine, and sanitary sewers (not to mention tools, technology, and manpower). Nevertheless, the work is incredibly rewarding, say those involved.

Hard Workers Make Good Hires

Eric S. Steinhauser, PE, of Sanborn, Head & Associates, says his company is always on the lookout for college grads who are willing to work hard.

"It's really hard to hire good, qualified engineers that have a desire to work hard," he says. "We want to hire people who are smart, who have a desire to learn, and who have an interest in the bigger picture of what they're doing."

Sanborn, Head & Associates, with offices in New England, the Midwest, and the United Kingdom, employs 80 professionals— mostly in the field of geo-environmental and geo-technical services.

"There's a lot of field work and drilling and sampling activities and learning your first five years," he says. "When you come out of school, you work on individual tasks but as your career develops, you will get to manage projects."

You can find EWB collegiate groups on campus, and participating in an EWB project can change forever those dull "what I did on my summer vacation" essays.

As important as the work is, however, EWB project manager Rick Strittmater, PE, says it probably should not be the first choice of a career location upon graduation.

"I'd go to a private company," he says emphatically. "I wouldn't even go to the government.

"In the government you could end up being pigeonholed in a job you hate. There are a lot of engineers out there who have spent a lot of their careers checking concrete culvert under county bridges."

Strittmater believes strongly that new engineers should move quickly toward receiving their Professional Engineer designation and that's a lot easier with a private company than anywhere else.

"To earn a PE, one of the things you need is to have the supervision of someone who already is a licensed Professional Engineer. A lot of times you're not going to get that with a government job.

"In a private company, you have a much better chance of having someone looking over your shoulder. You're going to be making that company a lot of money (through your work) but while you're working for them, they're dumping water all over you. They're helping you grow. You're working on a lot of different projects and, in a really big outfit, you may be working with a thousand other engineers."

Strittmater also says that working with a large engineering company would not preclude the new engineer from participating in EWB projects around the world. "There are a number of large companies that are members. People from those companies may be loaned to us for a project and then they go back," he said.

CHAPTER 13

Around the World

How a global economy and U.S. trends will affect you

"Don't worry about people stealing your ideas. If your ideas are any good, you'll have to ram them down people's throats."

–Howard Aiken, IBM engineer

A U.S. company can hire 11 young professional engineers in India for the cost of one in America.

Are you wondering what this has to do with you?

If you're going to pursue engineering, then you need to know about its "foreign factors" (and they extend far beyond the unsettling factoid above) and how they will undoubtedly change the future of engineering employment right here in the United States for years to come.

"Engineering today is in fact global. When you are an engineer, you will partner with people in other parts of the world to develop products and systems," says Dr. David Wormley, president-elect of the American Society for Engineering Education and Penn State's dean of engineering.

"We have a global economy where you can have partners around the world. It's important to understand other cultures and how other people think," he says.

Meanwhile, it is generally known that not enough Americans are being trained in science and technology and there are jobs in their fields—read that, engineering—that are going unfilled.

According to the National Academy of Engineering, the proportion of U.S. undergraduate students studying engineering is the lowest in the developed world at 4 to 5 percent. Compare that to most European countries, where the number is 12 to 13 percent, or to China, where the NAE estimates that more than 40 percent of the students are engaged in some form of engineering study.

Although there are national movements to try to improve the number of students studying science and technology in the United States, the situation today is particularly discouraging in the pre-college years. For example: about one-third of American fourth-graders and one-fifth of eighth-graders lack the competence to perform even basic mathematical computations, according to information NAE presented to Congress.

A recent poll showed that 68 percent of eighth-grade U.S. students were being taught math by teachers without degrees or even certification in math, and 93 percent of students in grades five through nine were learning science from teachers who lacked similar credentials.

Start Behind, Stay Behind

Engineering faculty members say they are seeing too many students with inferior math skills, some so far behind that they never can quite catch up enough to handle a demanding engineering curriculum and then graduate.

That, in turn, means fewer engineering graduates and a major problem for U.S. companies. For years, firms have relied on foreign-born engineers, trained both in the United States and in their home countries, to fill the gap. However, that talent pool may be shrinking due to tighter security restrictions in the United States and increased technology leading to more employment opportunities in their home nations.

Currently, nearly half of the engineers holding doctorates in America were born abroad, as were one-fourth of the engineering faculty members at U.S. colleges and universities. In addition, more than one-third of the Nobel Prizes awarded in the United States between 1990 and 2004 went to foreign-born scientists.

An American education is attractive, whether earned by a U.S. citizen or a foreign national. Eighteen of the world's 20 most prestigious research institutions are in the United States, for example. There is no doubt that a U.S.-based education will hold you in good stead here and when applying for jobs with foreign companies or U.S. companies abroad

That value of an American education also has not been lost on students born overseas. More than half of the engineering doctoral degrees (59.4 percent) awarded in 2005 were earned by foreign nationals and 42.6 percent of the master's degrees went to non-U.S. citizens, as did 7.5 percent of the undergraduate degrees.

Amid tighter security restrictions following 9/11, however, the United States has been issuing fewer visas for students and for science and engineering workers. The annual legal visas set aside for "highly qualified foreign workers" dropped from 195,000 per year down to 65,000. At the same time, U.S. law will grant a visa for foreign students to attend U.S. universities only if they promise to return home when they graduate.

So what's a company to do when—as we mentioned earlier—it can hire 11 engineers in India for the cost of just one here? Or, thanks to the Internet, it also can assign drafting, design, and other engineering tasks at lower cost to well-trained English-speaking engineers in countries like India, China, Korea, Russia, and the Philippines—and possibly have some of the tasks completed before the U.S. company reopens the next morning?

A Worrisome Development

It is not difficult to see why this foreign outsourcing, also known as offshore engineering, might be an attractive option. It's also not surprising that U.S. engineers find it alarming. The National Society for Professional Engineers and the Institute of Electrical and Electronics Engineers are among those that have issued position statements.

The NSPE believes offshore engineering should be used as a last resort when talent cannot be found in the United States, and any work should be completed following "the same rules, regulations, laws, and ethical codes that employers and employees are subject to in the U.S."

The Society also notes that some state engineering licensure boards are questioning the legality of "offshore work" not performed under the "responsible charge" of a licensed Professional Engineer. In Florida, for example, "responsible charge" requires the physical presence of a Professional Engineer.

The IEEE statement says offshore outsourcing already is contributing to "unprecedented levels of unemployment among American electrical, electronics, and computer engineers," and even poses a long-term challenge to U.S. military and homeland security. Many other scientists and engineers also are concerned about how offshore engineering will impact American jobs and whether there can be assurances that engineering done around the world will meet U.S. standards.

"Offshore engineering does cut into the job market," says National Society of Professional Engineers President Kathryn Gray of Wheaton, Illinois. "However, typically that happens in the industrial field.

"It's not as prevalent in the design-build environment because of state licensure laws and the necessity for the folks who are in the engineering profession to be familiar with the codes—both the building codes and the code of ethics."

Congress Paying Attention

Be assured that "foreign factors" are more than theoretical musings. They are being discussed in the halls of Congress and most certainly represent hot-button topics for engineering organizations.

Some people believe the issues have roots in what some fear are disturbing indications that the United States may be losing its science and technology edge.

Consider some of these sobering statistics provided to Congress to accompany the 2006 report "Rising Above the Gathering

Storm: Energizing and Employing America for a Brighter Economic Future" by the National Academies' Committee on Prospering in the Global Economy of the 21st Century:

- In a recent international test involving mathematical understanding, U.S. students finished in 27th place among the nations participating.
- About two-thirds of the U.S. students studying chemistry and physics are being taught by teachers with no major or certificate in those subjects. In the case of math taught in grades 5 through 12, the fraction is one-half.
- High school seniors in the United States rank in the bottom 10 percent among their international peers.
- The United States today is a net importer of high technology products. The U.S. share of global high-tech exports has fallen in the last two decades from 30 percent to 17 percent, while America's trade balance in high-tech manufactured goods shifted from a *positive* $33 billion in 1990 to a *negative* $24 billion in 2004.

The National Science Board, in its most recent "Science and Engineering Indicators" report, also cited a troubling decline in the number of U.S. citizens training to be engineers and scientists, saying it represents "an urgent and critical problem of the science and engineering labor force." The board predicted that if trends continue:

1. The number of jobs in the U.S. economy that require science and engineering training will grow (growth has been about 5 percent annually, compared to 1 percent for the remainder of the labor force).
2. The number of U.S. citizens prepared for those jobs will, at best, be level.
3. The availability of people from other countries who have science and engineering training will decline, either because of limits to entry imposed by U.S. national security restrictions or because of intense global competition for people with these skills.

"Even if action is taken today to change these trends, the reversal is 10 to 20 years away," the report says. "The students entering the science and engineering workforce in 2004 with advanced degrees decided to take the necessary math courses to enable this career path when they were in middle school, up to 14 years ago.

"The students making that same decision in middle school today won't complete advanced training for science and engineering occupations until 2018 or 2020."

The Board expressed concern that without action today, in 2020 the nation could find "the ability of U.S. research and education institutions to regenerate has been damaged and that their preeminence has been lost to other areas of the world."

This is one reason why so many engineering groups have launched K–12 science and technology outreach efforts to students, parents, and teachers. National groups also are calling for U.S. leaders to take steps to shore up our efforts in science and technology.

Craig Barrett, chairman of the National Academy of Engineering, told the group's 2005 meeting that the United States for the past two decades has spent roughly $5 billion annually on basic research in the physical sciences—less than Intel Corporation, IBM, and Microsoft each spend in a year.

"Ironically, the United States spends roughly $25 billion a year on agricultural subsidies, five times the amount we spend on basic R&D in physical sciences. Is it better to fund the industries of the 19th Century than the industries of the 21st Century?" he asked.

Meanwhile, a recent Duke University study painted a somewhat more positive picture of U.S. science and technology, noting:

- almost one-third of the world's science and engineering researchers are employed in the United States;
- 35 percent of science and engineering articles are published in America; and
- the United States accounts for 40 percent of the globe's research and development expenditures.

If engineering is your chosen field, the issues facing science and technology will affect you. It's also important to be aware of the global landscape and how all of these factors could impact your employment future.

An American Working for the Japanese in Vietnam

Twenty-five years after the Vietnam War, Professional Engineer Rick Strittmater found himself in Hanoi, working for a Japanese company that had won a contract to help rebuild the bombed-out bridges around the city.

"The funny thing was, the Ministry of Transportation hired the Japanese company to do the work, but when the Japanese got there, they were told they had to do everything according to American standards. The Japanese didn't know anything about American standards, so they ended up hiring me.

"I was teaching the Japanese engineers, who were teaching the Vietnamese contractor.

"After the first couple of bridges were done, the Japanese left and the Vietnamese asked me to stay and continue to teach their people."

Strittmater, who today is a project manager with Engineers Without Borders, says working around the world is an eye-opening experience. "A designer might be able to draw a picture of a project, but that doesn't mean you can build it. Not everybody in the world has the same kind of equipment we have here in the United States. Sometimes you find yourself being pretty resourceful."

CHAPTER 14

Getting Licensed

An essential career move?

"One has to watch out for engineers–they begin with the sewing machine and end up with the atomic bomb."

–*Marcel Pagnol*
Critiques des Critiques

L ike everything else in engineering, it pays to think ahead a little about whether you someday may want to get a license and become a "Professional Engineer."

Did you just scream and start pulling your hair out? We're not surprised.

Let's face it: We already suggested that you need to plot your high school education to include a certain number of math and science courses just to get into a good engineering program.

Then we told you that you have to complete an academically rigorous curriculum to get a good job once you get out of college.

Now we're telling you that as soon as you graduate from college, you need to start thinking about becoming a licensed Professional Engineer (PE).

Well, that's not exactly true.

We're actually suggesting that the time for you to start thinking about becoming a Professional Engineer is before you graduate from college. In fact, we suggest you take the Fundamentals of Engineering (FE) exam (also called the Engineer-in-Training exam) midway through your senior year because your coursework still will be fresh in your mind.

Before we get to that, let's talk about why you may want to become a licensed Professional Engineer.

Who Must Be Licensed?

The truth is you don't need a license to be an engineer and, in fact, roughly 75 percent of the people out there working for engineering firms today are not licensed. For certain things you may want to do in your career, however, a license is mandatory.

For instance, only licensed engineers can prepare, approve (sign and seal), and submit engineering plans to public authorities. That means if you or your company want to build a sewer plant or a water tower for a city, a jail for the county, or a highway for the state or federal governments—any project that involves the taxpayers' money—you must be a licensed engineer. Even beyond government work, almost any project of considerable size, scope, and expense is going to require that someone who can prove he or she is responsible draw and approve the plans. Part of that proof is a license.

If you hope to head your own company someday, or even be a consultant when you retire in the distant future, a license will serve as verification that you know what you're doing. If you ever plan to teach engineering, more and more schools are requiring that instructors be licensed.

Even beyond that, of course, is the fact that a license shows you've taken an interest in your career and that you are ambitious and dedicated enough to want to excel. That's the sort of thing that can lead to quicker promotions, new opportunities, and more money.

"If you don't get licensed as a civil engineer, you're really limiting your employment prospects," says Gregory Bovid, a PE with Ayres & Associates in Midland, Michigan, and chairman of the Michigan Board of Engineer Licensing.

"You can probably work in certain industrial settings—possibly maintaining facilities. And if you're in the private sector where you're not working with public dollars, you can probably find jobs.

"Even some municipalities and counties will hire engineers who are not licensed, but their capability of rising through the ranks—their possibilities of promotion—are pretty limited. And that, of course, limits income."

In addition, he emphasizes, the time to take that road to higher professionalism is before you're out of college. "The FE is a review of your four years of college. You need to do it while you still remember it," he suggests.

The "PE" after your name also could open employment doors to you that might be closed to the 75 percent who don't seek licensure. In times of layoffs and changing corporate priorities, a PE could help keep you from losing your job, or help find a new one more quickly.

On the downside, however, you should also be aware that more states are seeing a continual need to upgrade the knowledge base of their Professional Engineers. In other words, as the engineering profession develops new ways to do old things (and even newer ways to do new things), states want their licensed Professional Engineers to stay current. This means in many states, licensed engineers should expect to take additional classroom hours on an annual, biannual, or tri-annual basis for the rest of their lives to keep their licenses active.

While continuing education—"continuing professional competency," or CPC, as many states call it—is not necessarily expensive, when you consider that many engineers are licensed in several states and that each of those states could approve different CPC requirements, you could be very busy just keeping your license intact.

How Do You Become a Professional Engineer?

There are only four steps:

First, education: Most states require you to have, minimally, a four-year degree in engineering from an ABET-accredited program in order to become a Professional Engineer. Requirements vary from state to state, however, so be sure to check with your state licensing board. Many states allow college students to take the FE (Fundamentals of Engineering) exam before they graduate, during their junior or senior year of college.

Second, you have to pass the Fundamentals of Engineering exam (or "Engineer-in-Training" test—various states have different names for it, but the test is the same and it is administered and graded by the National Council of Examiners for Engineering and Surveying). We'll discuss the test—and what it takes to pass it—in just a moment.

Third, you have to gain experience under the supervision of someone who already is a licensed PE. In most cases, you will need at least four years of supervised experience and you should keep a log of your work, including the task, the name of the client, the name of your supervisor, and other data. The licensing board will want to review that diary later.

Individual states have different requirements. Michigan, for instance, requires that you work under at least three PEs on different projects to be eligible to sit for the PE exam. Also, some states require engineering practice beyond the initial four years for those who have not graduated from an engineering program accredited by ABET.

Fourth, you have to take the Principles and Practice of Engineering exam (the PE exam) that the NCEES also administers and scores.

The FE Exam

Even if you're not sure you want to pursue your PE license, taking the Fundamentals of Engineering/Engineer-in-Training exam while you're still in college is a good idea. In fact, some schools treat the exam as a graduation requirement for engineering students.

The FE/EIT consists of two four-hour sessions. There are 120 general engineering education questions on the first part of the test, given in the morning. That test covers things like engineering terms, equations, concepts, methods, and typical problems. Questions will involve mathematics, chemistry, computers, statics and dynamics, electric circuits, thermodynamics, and a host of other things that, generally speaking, are covered in the first couple of years of undergraduate engineering study.

The afternoon test has a somewhat different character. There are 60 questions more focused on specific engineering disciplines, you get to choose which discipline you want to take. In other words, a student at one desk may be answering questions relevant to chemical engineering while a student at the next desk may be answering questions about mechanical engineering. Specific branch exams available in the afternoon are: chemical, civil, electrical, environmental, general, industrial, and mechanical.

All of the questions on the FE/EIT are multiple-choice. In terms of scoring, the NCEES takes your raw score of correct answers or points and translates them into a scaled score. In general, examinees need a scaled score of 70 or higher to pass the exam. You do not receive your numerical score, only whether you passed or failed the exam. Examinees who fail receive a diagnostic report of their strong and weak topic areas to help them focus their study if they choose to take the exam again. Overall, usually at least two-thirds of those taking the FE will pass it the first time. Any student who doesn't pass the test the first time is welcome to take it again.

There is no "federal engineer" license. It's all on the state level, but all states administer the FE/EIT and PE exams and recognize the pass/fail scores determined by NCEES, so your license is generally portable from one state to another.

After you pass the exam, you are classified as an engineering intern (EI) or engineer-in-training (EIT).

If you are in an engineering school, the school should know when your state will be offering the FE/EIT exam. Otherwise, check the NCEES Web site (*www.NCEES.org*) for a schedule. Typically, the exams are twice a year—in October and April.

Preparing for the Exams

While some exam candidates prefer to review for the FE and PE exams on their own, many find that a guided review of some kind is immensely helpful in focusing their time and energy. For the FE, some colleges and universities offer inexpensive review courses over a period of weeks before the exam date. Various professional organizations also offer PE review courses.

Another form of guided review is an exam preparation book focused on the topics and types of questions you are likely to encounter on the exam. Kaplan AEC Education publishes exam prep books for the FE and PE exams, including complete sample exams to help you gauge your areas of strength and weakness. For more information, visit *www.kaplanaecengineering.com*.

The PE Exam

After you've passed the FE and worked under a licensed Professional Engineer for the amount of time required by your state, you may decide to go ahead and take the Principles and Practice Exam to obtain your license. While criteria change from time to time, basically the PE exam lasts eight hours and is divided into a morning and afternoon session.

PE exams are available for a wide range of engineering disciplines, and you should take the exam that applies to your field of practice. With the exception of the Structural II exam, all exams are multiple-choice and consist of 80 to 100 questions. The exams are "open book" tests, although some states have restrictions on what kinds of references you may bring into the exam.

After you pass the PE exam, you may have some additional requirements for licensure depending on the requirements of your state. Your state licensing board provides this information; often it is easily accessible via a Web site.

CHAPTER 15

This Inventive Thing

Your big idea and how to fund it

Architects and engineers are among the most
fortunate of men since they build their own
monuments with public consent, public approval
and often public money.
                    –John Prebble, The High Girders

T his chapter is kind of an aside to your development as an engineer and simply acknowledges the possibility that— regardless of where you are in your education—you may already have something in mind that you would like to develop and bring to the marketplace. A lot of engineers are inventors, and you need only go to the U.S. Patent and Trademark Office to prove it.

While not frequent, it also is not altogether rare that someone of high school age already will have developed a new computer game. A child in middle school came up with an idea for a jacket to carry Beanie Babies.

A later chapter (Chapter 19) discusses the possibility—even likelihood—that you could find yourself working on a research project in school that actually has some money-making applications in the real world and we'll talk about the circumstances under which you might benefit from that enterprise.

In this chapter, however, we wanted to give you a short overview of the inventive process and how ideas often come to market.

As patent lawyer Robert Fieseler of McAndrews, Held & Malloy in Chicago points out, having a great idea is not the same as having a great product—and having a great idea and a great product still doesn't amount to much unless you get the money to put it in front of the public. Fieseler says the way things typically move from the idea stage to the commercially marketable stage is pretty straightforward.

Raising Money

Let's say you have an idea and you talk to a couple of your friends about it. They think it's a good idea and they're willing to help you develop it.

The first thing you need is for the four of you to pull together enough cash to get the idea off the ground. If you're a student, you may ask your parents for money, and they and your friends may have other resources they can tap.

"So you raise as much money as you can," Fieseler says. "Part of that money is going to go to a provisional patent application ($100 government filing fee). But you're also going to want a patent attorney to do a state-of-the-art search for you to find out if others already have patented something that is similar to what you have in mind.

"Remember, one of the important things about a patent search is that it also turns up all the ideas like yours that didn't work. You don't want to throw away a lot of money only to come up with the same failure that somebody else had."

Depending on the search, an attorney could cost a couple of thousand dollars.

Let's assume your idea is unique and you decide to go forward. The next step might be for you and the other patent owners to rent some small space in an industrial park where you can develop your invention.

Finding Influential Backers

"The next thing you're doing is talking to other people who already are in the business your idea applies to. You're explaining to them what your invention does and why it's needed. You're showing them your drawings, maybe you have a PowerPoint presentation. What you are looking for is an 'angel investor' who will fund you to get your invention to the next level. Usually, you're looking for angel investors to provide $1 million to $5 million."

What are they getting for their money? "Those investors are taking stock in your company."

By now you probably have filed for some additional patents on your device and word should be getting out that you may have "The Next Big Thing."

The next step, says Fieseler, is to find private investors who—depending on your invention, of course—could bring your funding up to $10 million or $15 million.

"Remember, by the time you have brought in a private investor, you have moved a long way from you at the dining room table or four guys in a garage. You now may have a hundred people with stock in your company.

"You need to make sure that you or the original four guys have your interests adequately protected. You may not be making all the critical decisions at this point. In fact, your private investors are only there to make money. They may already be talking to the largest companies in your industry to see if they want to buy out your product. If you haven't protected yourself with patents and legal contracts, you could have your idea sold out from under you. That sort of thing happens."

Bear in mind here that being bought out by a larger company isn't always a bad thing. It is not unusual for the primary inventor to take a product so far, and then let others with more experience or technological know-how take over and make it commercial.

Developing Ideas

Also, of course, bear in mind that partnering up with a large company often means bringing the product to market much faster. Large companies can help prove the concept, work out any bugs, and will typically have sales forces in place to begin the cash flow.

Students should know that many universities now have "incubator" programs that facilitate a lot of the early work in refining products and moving them to market. One of the earliest of those programs is the Advanced Technology and Development Center at Georgia Tech, which provided support for MindSpring (now Earthlink) during its developmental phase in the mid '90s, among other things.

Some of these incubator programs are very well-funded and well-connected within the industries they serve.

If you've watched what you're doing, made sure you documented your refinements along the way, and had clear understandings and legal contracts with those you're doing business with, you should be all right.

Start with a Big Idea

"Mosquitoes were so thick you get a mouthful with every breath," wrote a worker on the Panama Canal, arguably one of the greatest engineering challenges in the last 100 years.

However, the U.S. Army Corps of Engineers' construction of the waterway contributed far more to mankind than a 50-mile ditch. There was the creation of new technology to lift and lower the mammoth ships as they moved through the locks, the development of huge electric generators to manipulate the gates, the carving of a railroad across the mountains, and the building of whole cities to house nearly 45,000 workers.

To deal with the malaria and yellow fever, teams of biologists and medical researchers harvested reams of data linking insects to disease, and there was the development of new controls as well as new medicines that the world would soon use.

The price: $375 million and 5,600 lives lost to disease and accident.

A New York newspaper wrote years later upon the death of chief engineer George Washington Goethals: "It would be impossible to overstate what he has done. It is the greatest task of any kind that any man in the world has accomplished ... it is the greatest task of its own kind that has ever been performed in the world at all."

CHAPTER 16

Computers in Engineering

Who needs you?

The good news: Computers allow us to work 100% faster. The bad news: They generate 300% more work.

—Unknown

Computers are integral to every engineering discipline. They can help engineers determine how much traffic a bridge can carry or whether a building will survive an earthquake.

They can generate specifications for machine parts or installing electrical systems. They are used for quality control, to make systems and processes more efficient, and even to mimic the human body.

There is no doubt that computers have dramatically changed the engineering profession and will continue to alter it in ways we cannot even imagine today. They already can do trillions of math equations in a fraction of a second, but even that will seem slow in the future.

In the mid-1970s computers began to be widely used in the engineering industry following the development of programs using mathematical equations to analyze complex structural problems. Then came computer-aided design (CAD) and 3D models. The rest is history.

Now that computers are here, and can do so many things, does the world still need engineers?

On the Job

Ed Richardson, manager of engineering for the mammoth international engineering company Bechtel headquartered in San Francisco, cautions there are many positives about computers in engineering, but some risks as well.

"Computers allow us to do analysis much faster," he says. "A hundred years ago we did calculations by hand, 75 years ago we did them with slide rules, and now we do them with computers. You can get answers much more quickly. And you can calculate more accurately.

"In the old days, if I was doing a load analysis on a beam, I'd calculate what I need and set a wide margin for error. With computers we can model more precisely. Instead of 10 tons of steel, maybe I'd only need 8 tons. We can make sure things fit more properly. We can do the calculations much faster, and we can save on materials."

Nevertheless, the ability to save on materials is both good news and bad news. With things like support beams now built to computer specifications, the computer better be right because the margin of safety has been reduced dramatically.

And that's a problem, says Richardson.

"People always believe what the computer tells them—whether it's right or wrong. I could walk into a meeting with my slide rule and people would ask how I calculated my answers. But I remember once when I walked in with a four-inch high stack of computer printouts and nobody doubted anything I said. People don't question (computers) nearly enough. There is something inherently unhealthy about that."

At Bechtel, he said, engineers are told to come up with the answer first and then ask the computer.

"I want our people to know about what the answer is going to be," he said. "So if the computer's answer is a lot different than yours, you can go back and figure out where the error was. Sometimes it's in the computer."

Again on the upside, however, computers have made possible work-sharing on a global scale. "Engineers in New Delhi can be working on the same modeling project as the people in London and Texas. Computers allow for an exchange of data that lowers the cost of doing business. They allow you to automate steps and cut out repetition. That cuts out a lot of laborious calculation," Richardson says.

However, that could ultimately lead to less collaboration between humans.

"You're moving a lot of data around, but you're not sitting elbow-to-elbow with people working on the same project. Different people have different expectations and different attitudes about what you're working on. They have different attitudes about risk and rewards, and legal issues. In the United States, innovation can bring huge rewards. In other places, you may be punished for taking risks. Those kinds of understanding and viewpoints are going to be missing."

All in all, however, Richardson dismisses the notion that computers will someday do all engineering work.

"Engineering hasn't changed in thousands of years," he says. "We've changed the tools and our ability to work with people around the world. But we need engineers to make decisions, to visualize, to create, and innovate."

Kathryn Gray, a licensed Professional Engineer who founded GrayTech Software Inc. in Wheaton, Illinois, in 1983, echoes that sentiment.

"Engineering software is a tool, just like any other tool that you use—a ruler, a calculator. It takes someone with the appropriate talent to know what to do with that tool," she says.

"You can't give a two-year-old a hammer and expect the same quality of workmanship in building a table as you would if you gave it to a carpenter. It's the same thing with software," says Gray. "It's just like using a calculator or a slide rule to help you in your computations. You still have to acquire an understanding of the process and anticipate the result."

Gray also says that when an engineer plans a project or designs something, he or she will think through all of the possibilities that go into the project, "but the computer goes through the detailed calculations."

Like Richardson, Gray believes having a computer on the desk does not mean the person in front of it can be less talented. Adds

Soha Hassoun, a computer science engineering professor at Tufts University, "The bottom line is they have to know as much as they did before or more. One of the big issues with computers is: How do you know the computer got the right answer?"

Hassoun agrees that computers complement the work of engineers; they don't replace them.

"When you think about some of the tasks that are being automated, they are the dull, mundane, and error-prone tasks," she says. "Now the time it takes to design something has shrunk significantly.

"One of the most important things is that with the computer you are able to build computer models and simulations of what you can build," she says.

Keith Morris, president of an Apex, North Carolina, firm that manufactures robotic parts for industrial automation, says engineers still need strong math backgrounds even with computers as a tool.

"If you're going to design something or calculate the stress on a piece of machinery, you still have to know how to work the formula," says Morris. "People say, why take calculus, you never use it, but a lot of math concepts help you think and understand better."

In the Classroom

Meanwhile, engineering educators also want their students to understand that while the computer is a tool and it can do wonderful things, engineering knowledge is still necessary for it to work correctly. Students who use the computer as a crutch, plugging in numbers until they get a conclusion they cannot later defend, will not be furthering their education.

If thus far you've only used computers to communicate with friends over the Internet, play games, or to do your homework, you will be amazed at what computers can do in the engineering profession. You will encounter programs with names you have never have heard of before and a variety of software that can even help you design experiments, build models, and simulate vibrations.

There will be programs to analyze data and make graphs. You may even do your own programming to solve complicated problems requiring multiple repeated computations.

An electrical engineering student might use software that creates schematics, designs circuit layouts, and even simulates the circuits themselves. An architectural engineer could use a computer to analyze structures, lighting, and building environments. In addition, there are programs to do cost analyses and monitor the performance of manufacturing processes.

For civil engineering students, computers can replace tedious mechanical drawing tasks, as well as do structural analysis and design. Mechanical engineering students also can use computer programs for design, as well as to study fluid dynamics and simulate mechanical vibrations, for example.

Computers can take you to whole new worlds in the field of engineering, but you need to drive the car rather than just go along for a computer-simulated ride.

Garbage In, Garbage Out

Jeff Drake, a structural PE and project manager with Ambrose Engineering Inc., in Cedarburg, Wisconsin, reminds us that computers are only as good as the data that goes into them.

"It's still necessary to provide input for computer programs to generate information," he warns. "That information has to come from competent people educated in engineering principles and those with exposure to the (appropriate) industry. Garbage in, garbage out.

"Computers are nothing more than intelligent tools that are necessary to compete in this high-tech field."

CHAPTER 17

What Else You Need to Know

Being well-rounded for success

"Engineering students have no life, and can prove it mathematically."

—*Anonymous*

I n the old days, the engineer pretty much had a reputation of spending countless hours behind a desk, peering over a set of designs, and trying to figure out how to do something better, or trying to find the flaw that meant something didn't work at all.

Deservedly or not (and probably not), engineers had reputations as being dull nerds and loners, isolationists. People who worked around the clock behind locked doors, telling other people to go away; not "team players" and not very interesting people.

If that does describe you, however, you might consider overhauling your personality and start digging through your soul for additional talents. In today's world, no one is an island.

The modern engineer is faced with a broad range of chores, all of which are going to connect to engineering, but many of which may stretch beyond his or her core competency. For instance, your boss may expect you to understand the economics of the project you're working on and where it fits into the larger organization.

In this day and age, no one is likely to give you a blank check and say, "Build it and they will come." More likely, the phrase will be "Build it, bring it in on time and under budget, and then we'll turn it over to marketing."

To do that, of course, means you're going to need a little bit of background in cost/benefit analysis, return on investment, cash flow analysis and, who knows, a little bit of labor relations probably wouldn't hurt.

If You're an Engineer, You're in Business

Before launching ATI Industrial Automation in Apex, North Carolina, Keith Morris worked for a company in a division that made devices used by industrial robots. When the company decided to sell off that division because of its poor profit margin, he and some of his fellow engineers decided to buy it.

"There were 35 people and they had $1 million in sales. There was no way it could be profitable with that kind of ratio. We cut the 35 down to 10 and we became barely profitable," he said.

"We were all engineers. We had no business background. We tried and failed, and learned the hard way how to run a business. We had to learn marketing and deal with HR issues. As we figured things out, the sales kept going up. Now, after 18 years, we have $20 million in annual sales."

Morris believes engineering schools could and should offer at least basic business courses. "They don't have to go into advanced details. But it's important to know how to do an income statement and a balance sheet."

In fact, many schools are reducing core course requirements in engineering (and other science majors) so that students can take advantage of courses outside of their main discipline, such as in business, philosophy, and sociology, to help round out the individual student. State-funded universities especially tend to insist on a mix that will include at least some liberal arts courses along with math and the sciences.

Even those lowly English classes are proving important—and usable once you have begun your career. To some, the new watchwords of the industry are "If you didn't write it up, it never happened."

If you cannot literately convey your team's results, successes, or failures to your colleagues in a way they can understand and build upon, your research and developments are nearly useless.

Broaden Your Education

As a result of some universities broadening their engineering undergraduate curriculums, they have shifted some formerly undergraduate courses to postgraduate school.

Ed Richardson, manager of engineering at Bechtel and a member of the board of advisors at U.C. Berkeley and California State Polytechnic University, says the undergraduate requirements there have fallen from 140–150 hours to 120–130. "They're getting less engineering coursework than they used to, but a lot of them are making that up by going into master's programs."

Nevertheless, the bottom line is he is happy with the engineers coming out of schools. "The young engineers we're seeing today are energetic and articulate," he says. "I find they are comfortable working in any age group of people. They are very comfortable expressing their views. We (Bechtel) are very happy with the new engineers we're seeing."

Travel the World, Make a Difference

Eric S. Steinhauser of Concord, New Hampshire, a senior associate principal with Sanborn, Head & Associates, a multidisciplinary firm providing geo-environmental and geotechnical services worldwide, says engineering offers opportunities to see the world while practicing a fulfilling craft.

"I like the diversity of my practice," he says. "In consulting engineering, you get to work with lots of people, travel to places you might not have been before, try new things, and look at research and try to implement new things. I also like the fact that you have a broad impact, although it might not be noticeable right away.

"In other professions, results can happen in a relatively quick time period. But when you're an engineer, the projects you work on—like providing for safe waste disposal or building a bridge—can impact many lives.

"You may not see the result right away, but it's very important for our society to have these things built, and constructed safely."

The Importance of People Skills

Reversing a bad reputation

"I can't understand it. I can't even understand the people who can understand it."
—Queen Juliana of the Netherlands

This chapter isn't filled with new information as much as it is a review of what you already know. Here's what it says: "It takes all kinds." "Different strokes for different folks." "You need to work and play well with others."

If you're clear on those concepts, especially as they apply to the engineering workplace, feel free to skip the next few pages. If you're not quite sure what we're driving at, however, you might want to read on just a little bit more.

As we discussed in the previous chapter, engineers generally have reputations of being "antisocial" ("hostile," "arrogant," "elitist," fill in your own derogatory cliché here) individuals who would rather be left alone to do their work than be involved with, well, the rest of humanity. They are confident of their own ability to find a solution, and less confident in the ability of others. While it's true that all stereotypes are wrong, there often is a little truth in even the worst of characterizations.

Al Gray, executive director of the National Society of Professional Engineers, concedes to carrying a slide rule in his pocket through much of his high school and college careers. He maintains that budding engineers aren't really "different" from other kids, it's just that their focus tends to be more academic and less social than their peers.

So the stereotypes are untrue?

He shrugs, "Maybe not completely."

A Better Image

The problem is that while a young person can get away with a "loner" image in high school and maybe even to some extent in college, once you get into the workplace, isolation simply doesn't work anymore.

John MacGinnis, chief engineer for the Portsmouth Naval Shipyard in Kittery, Maine, that employs 400 engineers, says he wishes he had learned more "people skills" along with his engineering skills at the U.S. Merchant Marine Academy as an undergraduate and later as a graduate student elsewhere.

"The hardest thing that they didn't teach, that you wish you had, were skills with dealing with people," says MacGinnis. "You really get no people skills for dealing with other people and how to get work done through working with others.

"Most engineering—particularly where I work—is a team effort. For me, it's a team effort between engineers and tradespeople, the mechanics who know how to get things done the fastest, cheapest way. We spend so much time working in teams, even as engineers, when we try to troubleshoot problems. We've got to work in teams and we're more effective as teams. You can get more out of a group as the sum rather than all the parts."

Indeed, in the modern corporation, everybody needs to be able to work with everybody else. "Teamwork" is the phrase of the day—cooperation and collegiality are now the watchwords of industry.

This means you are going to have to work well with the lawyers who negotiate the contracts and timelines for the products you build.

It means you are going to have to be diplomatic with the accountants who don't want to give you enough money to fund your project.

It means you are going to have to be polite to the artists who design the packages and the marketers who are going to try to oversell your invention.

All of these people have an important role to play in the success of the company you work for—which is to say, all those people have a role to play in your success.

The problems aren't so much the viewpoints of those other people but how they arrive at them, according to many engineers.

A Different Way of Thinking

Again, perspective is everything.

Engineers, for instance, are accustomed to finding "the" answer to a problem by reaching the end of a mathematical equation. It either calculates or it doesn't.

Lawyers, on the other hand, are more interested in finding "an" answer, rather than "the" answer. To many lawyers, the world is defined by shades of gray with any number of ways to arrive at a satisfactory solution. Compromise not only is common, but the rule.

Likewise, accountants constantly complain superiors are on their backs to protect the corporation's bottom line. Protect it from whom? You. The phrase "money is no object" is never heard in the modern corporation. The same is true for artists and marketers who rarely believe the talents they bring to their companies are rewarded, or even recognized. The marketing department never believes a product will "sell itself" (and they're probably right).

While we could offer you all sorts of stroking and suggest that you probably have the highest IQ of the bunch, at the end of the day what it comes down to is that you are going to have to live with other people's expertise in the sale of your efforts.

You are going to have to learn to speak to other people in terms they understand, and sometimes you are even going to have to write your results down—literally and legibly.

It's the way the world works.

Life Isn't Fair

Having said all that, however, there likely will be others in your environment that don't seem to play fair, and they may not even realize it.

They are architects, scientists, and others who are fundamental to the problem-solving portion of a project, just as you are as the engineer.

Back in the opening of this book, we pondered the question of how you would feel if a building you built won a prize, but it was the architect who appeared on the cover of *Newsweek*.

Likewise, how would you like it if you built a new particle accelerator but all the glory went to the scientists who discovered the principle? As American engineer Gordon Glegg wrote, "A scientist can discover a new star, but he cannot make one. He would need an engineer for that."

These are not rare situations.

Engineers rarely get credit for the good things they are involved with. That does not make scientists and architects the "bad guys" in any business proposition, but it does cause some friction.

People like NSPE's Al Gray insist there is no real rift between scientists and engineers, or between engineers and architects.

"At the university, architects tend to have a creative and art-inspired image," he says. "Engineers tend to have a much more staid, conservative image, sometimes projected by the often referenced pocket protector. That kind of gives one a feeling for where each is coming from.

"Architects are always tuned to the aesthetics of a project, but the engineers must provide the structural design and constructability and ultimately ensure that public health and safety

Part of the Team

John MacGinnis, chief engineer at the Portsmouth Naval Shipyard in Kittery, Maine, says what motivates him is the teamwork of engineering.

"What I most enjoy about engineering is the opportunity to work with other engineers, with similar educations but diverse backgrounds and experiences, in solving engineering problems," he says.

"There are always multiple ways to solve engineering problems. The best ideas and solutions, though, come out of engineering team dynamics; literally taking those ideas and blending them to solve the problem in the most efficient and successful way. It's synergy in action."

is protected. This can lead to some dispute over the authority to sign and seal plans and design documents.

"There can be overlapping of responsibilities," Gray said. "But as long as there is ongoing dialogue between the architect and engineers, there usually isn't a problem."

In many colleges, he adds, engineers are taking more architectural courses and architects are taking engineering classes.

Of a more frustrating nature, however, is how the public views scientists compared to how it views engineers. "We (engineers) frequently object to seeing great accomplishments attributed to scientists when in fact they are talking about an engineering project," Gray says.

"Scientists study and discover new physical, chemical, and biological relationships, and refine existing ones. But engineers create what does not exist to enhance our quality of life. What may be possible in the research would is not always practical in the real world, so scientists are in a different place than engineers."

"I don't think the public really understands what the scientist does. They often give scientists credit for what engineers do."

CHAPTER 19

Me and My Shadow: Engineers and Lawyers

The issues can begin in college

"The ancient Romans had a tradition: whenever one of their engineers constructed an arch, as the capstone was hoisted into place, the engineer assumed accountability for his work in the most profound way possible: he stood under the arch."
—*Michael Armstrong, former chairman of AT&T*

When you were a Cub Scout you delighted and amazed everyone by constructing a toothpick bridge that supported three tons of weight, and ever since then your parents wanted you to become an engineer and patent the process.

In college you fascinated a professor with your design and he worked with you to help refine it, but he left school midway through your senior year and went to work for a private construction company with millions of dollars worth of government highway contracts.

By the time you finished college, he was building "your" bridge all over the country.

There ought to be a law, you say? Well, there is. You just didn't know about it.

By nature and by definition, engineers tend to be inventors. Unfortunately, they tend not to be lawyers—and sometimes as you go through your career you are going to find that you need to be a little bit of both, and sometimes you need to be a lot of both.

In fact, you are going to find there are two basic times when you need to understand the legal atmosphere in which you work: One is when you are in school, and the other is when you're out.

When you are in school, you need to understand your rights when you and your research team discover the "Next Big Thing." When you are out of school, you need to understand your liability when your "Next Big Thing" is accused of not performing as promised or blamed for causing an injury.

In School

Before you read too much farther, it should be noted that blunt and honest conversation is an important element in any business relationship—and it is important to remember that occasionally your relationship with your university could be as much business as it is education.

Today, universities nationwide are earning hundreds of millions of dollars per year through licensing agreements with private companies based on research the university (its faculty and students) have performed. All this comes under the guise of "intellectual property."

If you are on a research team that is going to discover a new process or rewrite the laws of physics, you need to ask upfront who is going to own the product of your work—you, the university, or the private contractor who's paying for it—and whether you are entitled to any compensation. What you'll find is that all sorts of contracts are possible depending on who you are and your role in the research.

The bellwether legal case in all this is *United States v. Dubilier Condenser Corporation, 289 U.S. 178 (1933)*. The basics of the case were that Francis W. Dunmore and Percival D. Lowell were employees of the U.S. Bureau of Standards, working in the radio laboratories section. Their assignment was to work on "airplane radio problems."

While employees of the Bureau of Standards, they made a number of discoveries and patented them. The U.S. government sued them, contending they were government employees when they made the discoveries and therefore, the patents belonged to the United States. Dunmore and Lowell disagreed, saying their discoveries were only tangential to their "radio problem" research and therefore, the patents should belong to them. The government countered again, however, that the two were working on government time and in a government lab, using government equipment, and therefore, the patents belonged to the government.

The court essentially broke its decision into three parts:

1. If a contractor (in this case, the government) assigns a worker to create a new invention, then the contractor owns the invention and the worker only gets paid.
2. However, if a worker discovers something in the course of his research that is not directly related to his assigned work, then the worker may indeed claim the patent.
3. And if a worker discovers his invention while on someone else's time and using someone else's equipment, the owner of that time and equipment is entitled to a "shop-right," which the court defined as the right to use the invention or process in-house, but without being allowed to license the technology to others.

In the case of Dunmore and Lowell, the court awarded them the patents but granted the United States the shop-rights for their inventions. The importance of the case for any budding engineer is that the private sector and universities have adopted its general parameters as well.

As a research student, if you are under specific contract to come up with a new "Big Solution," the university or the contractor is probably going to own that solution. Alternatively, if you invent something as a by-product of your research, you may well be entitled to the patent.

If you made this discovery in a school lab or using school equipment, you may have to share shop-rights with the school.

Again, however, the best idea is to have a conversation with your faculty advisor or employer before you begin the research process.

As you can imagine, there are overlapping shades of gray in how subsequent courts have decided these issues and ultimately you may have to re-read whatever employment contracts you've signed to see if you've already surrendered any rights.

One quick caveat to remember: Big corporations and big universities have big legal departments dedicated to defending their rights, but not necessarily your rights. Again, the best idea is to have blunt conversations with your superiors before these questions arise, not afterward.

Patents, Trademarks, and Copyrights

Basically, there are three types of "intellectual property" that you may find yourself dealing with: Patents, trademarks, and copyrights. Here are some quick definitions.

A **patent** is something that is granted to an inventor that essentially does two things:

1. It allows the publication of your designs or processes so that others may see them. In the United States, we believe in pushing innovation forward, allowing others to see the "state of the art," and improve upon it if they can.
2. It grants the inventor a specific period—20 years—in which he or she may exclusively commercialize the invention or process, barring others during that time from copying the invention and developing a competing product.

If you'd like to patent something, go to the U.S. Patent and Trademark Office on the Web (*www.USPTO.gov*) and it will show you the steps. Be aware that there are various fees associated with patenting something. You'll likely spend at least $300 to $700 depending on what you are patenting, but you could easily spend twice that amount depending on whether you need a detailed patent search and if you need to hire an agent or attorney to do it.

A **trademark** (or **service mark**) is something you develop that helps the public identify that something is your work. A trademark prevents others from using a similar looking symbol or word to market their products in the hope of confusing the public.

Once you have a registered trademark with the Patent and Trademark Office, you may use the symbols "TM" (trademark) or "SM" (service mark) after the word or symbol.

Another option can be obtaining a state trademark for something sold only within a specific state and that fee may be a couple of hundred dollars. The fee for a federal trademark for things sold coast-to-coast is usually about $375. A trademark is good for ten years and is renewable for as long as you continue to market your product. Again, fees can go up depending on complexity and involvement of attorneys.

International trademarks also are available.

Copyrights usually pertain only to works of literature, music, dramatic presentations, choreography, pictures, sound recordings, and other forms of art. However, you may also copyright computer code.

Copyright is extended at the moment such works are created—no forms and no fees. However, if you truly want to protect your work in a court of law, you may want to register it, which simply establishes in a public record that you have created something. The fee for registering a copyright is $30. A copyright lasts for the duration of the author's life plus 70 years. For information see: *www.copyright.gov.*

Enough Jargon, What about *My* Invention?

Patent lawyer Robert Fieseler of McAndrews, Held & Malloy in Chicago (who earned his engineering degree from Rensselaer Polytechnic and became a Professional Engineer before heading to law school) points out first of all that anybody can obtain a patent on almost any invention, but that doesn't mean it will be commercially viable.

"Every Tuesday the Patent and Trademark Office may grant as many as 3,000 patents," he says. However, "out of the tens of thousands of patents granted each year, only a comparative handful ever make it to market."

Nevertheless, he adds, "If you're a big drug company, for instance, you may file for hundreds of patents per year. If just one of those proves to be commercially viable, you can make millions."

However, going back, if you are a Cub Scout with an amazing toothpick bridge, "The first thing you want to do is document your work. You want to take pictures. Keep all your paperwork. May sure everything is dated so you know what you developed and when you developed it."

Then you should file a provisional patent application.

"You don't need a lawyer to file a provisional patent application. You can do it with $100 with the U.S. Patent and Trademark Office and it's good for year."

Then when you get to college and attract the interest of a professor?

"When you start working with someone else, you need to document their contribution. Let's say that you have A that works pretty well, but the person you're working with comes up with B, and when A and B are put together, it works even better. At that point, you're going to file for another patent. And then, if some company expresses interest in your device and develops part C that makes it even better, then you get another patent.

"Since you're the inventor, you can do whatever you want with A, but if your first partner wants to sell A and B together, he needs to license it from you. Likewise, if you want to sell A and B together, you need his agreement to use part B. And the same with C."

It gets complicated, Fieseler said. By the time some inventions get to market, they could have a hundred different patents on them.

In the Workplace

Once you have an engineering job, not only will you likely deal with the previously mentioned legal restraints from time to time, but you'll also have to deal with others, depending on how high you climb the corporate ladder.

And no, you won't always have the company lawyer there to tell you what's right and what's wrong. A lot of times, it's going to be up to you to make a decision.

Linda K. Enghagen, an associate professor of law at the University of Massachusetts-Amherst, wrote the book *Fundamentals of Product Liability Law for Engineers,* which is considered one of the most important texts in the country on engineers and the law.

She points out that more and more, engineers are expected to be "compliance officers," as well as designers and builders.

"You have to be able to deal with contract specifications on the job," she says. "For instance, a lot of engineers end up working for companies that work within the defense industry—typically a private company with a government contract.

"Being the compliance officer means you will be responsible for specifics of the contract. You're going to be in charge of testing to make sure you've met government requirements. You're going to have to make sure those test results get to everybody who needs to see them.

"If there are delays, you are going to have to work with the company lawyers to negotiate contract extensions and penalties. A lot of these things lawyers can't do. They don't usually understand why something won't meet specifications, or why it's late or what a reasonable deadline would be. Those are things engineers know.

"When you get down to terms and conditions of the contract, the engineer is going to be the point person."

Enghagen believes universities do a generally lackluster job in preparing engineers for the paperwork involved in the realities of employment. "You don't anticipate how much of your time it's going to take."

Product liability also is of growing importance to engineers. "What engineers need to know is that just because you've designed something that is state of the art, that doesn't shield you from liability," she says.

In other words, the mere fact that you did everything you could to make a product work won't save you from prosecution if it harms the public.

Abraham Lincoln: Engineer?

A little known fact is that before he became a lawyer, politician, and president, Abraham Lincoln took a turn at engineering and obtained a patent for inventing a device for raising boats off river sandbars: A device for "Buoying Vessels Over Shoals."

Patent No. 6469, granted by the U.S. Patent Office on May 22, 1849, was for an inflatable pontoon that would fit along the sides of barges and lift them just high enough in the water to get them over shoals and shallow areas without having to unload their cargo.

The patent application included a detailed drawing and explanation of how the device worked. According to Lincoln's design, the multichambered pontoons could be partially or fully inflatable, depending on necessity, and would then be deflated and stored alongside when not in use.

History shows, however, that the device was never formally used.

She also points out there is an expanding field of law in software design. "If you've designed a piece of software and you say that it does 'X' but it turns out that it doesn't do it accurately, then it's defective," she said. "There is no difference between selling a lawn mower that is defective and a piece of software that is defective. Information technology is not insulated from product liability."

Another important area where engineers need to inject themselves these days is in the marketing of a new product. "You have to make sure that how you design a product and how it performs are accurately reflected in the sales literature that accompanies it," she says.

"If you've designed a product to do X, Y, and Z, but the marketing department says it does A, B, Q, and R, then there is going to be a problem."

More companies are including engineers on marketing teams specifically so that product "puffery" doesn't get out of hand. "It's one thing to say, 'My lawn mower is the best one on the market.' That's puffery. But if you misrepresent what the lawn mower does, that's something else."

The best advice, she suggests, is lots of conversations between the engineers, the marketing department, and the lawyers. You all need to have the same goal in mind.

The Ever-Ethical You

One decision could lose it all

What the engineer says: "Preliminary operational tests were inconclusive." What the engineer means: "The darn thing blew up when we threw the switch."

–Engineering blog

S o . . . the irony is that, although—as we've stated time and again—the foundation of your career will be built on your ability to do math and science, you could lose it all in the flash of a single decision that has little to do with either.

What we're talking about here is what you learned in kindergarten: the difference between right and wrong.

What we're talking about is ethics.

You got that lesson, you say? Got it from Mom and Dad a long time ago? You're good to go?

Terrific, then you'll breeze right through this chapter completely confident that you can make decisions that balance public safety against the loss of jobs (including your own) and the erosion of stockholder profits (to say nothing of the destruction of pension funds).

You'll be able to decide whether the long-term good should override a short-term evil.

You'll have no problem stopping a multimillion-dollar project dead in its tracks on the basis of a weld that looks curious to you, even though the veteran construction supervisor argues he's done a hundred projects with welds that look exactly like that and none of them have ever failed.

(And don't forget that at the end of his rant he called you a "pitiful, wet-behind-the-ears rookie" and he's managed to draw the attention of 50 laborers who are now standing still at a rate of $35 per hour, not to mention the drivers of five cement trucks who won't start pouring until you make a decision.)

What's your call?

Around the country, more engineers are being questioned about the decisions they make regarding all kinds of projects. You've read about some of those projects in the headlines: Questions about why levees fail, how tiles can fall off space shuttles, and even why whole sections of bridges or tunnels suddenly collapse.

Engineers are called before authorities who want to understand what the engineer said, who the engineer said it to, why a project was signed-off on, what objections might have been raised, and what the engineer could have done after his or her concerns were ignored. (Read that, "whistleblower.")

Moreover, these questions are asked in open forums with lawyers taking copious notes at the back of the room for class-action lawsuits to follow—maybe against your company.

How brave are you?

Even if you work on something that is not a spectacular failure and never sees a line of print in a newspaper, you could still be challenged for a myriad of other things: What caused the delays? Why was the cost so much higher? Why can't the building's air conditioners get the temperature below 90 degrees? Why can't the new eco-engine get the car above 70 miles per hour?

Again, the questions are going to be: What did you know? What did you say? What did you do? Why did you do it?

Codes of Ethics

Engineering and ethics are not the easy fit that you might think. At the end of this chapter we offer a handful of scenarios that each present tough decisions that individuals have to make, all weighted by a number of factors.

Of most interest, however, is that none of them is especially exotic. None is so rare that you might not be involved in an issue like it during the course of your career.

Ethics in engineering has become such a concern that many universities now offer ethics courses as part of their curriculums. Also, almost every professional engineering society, association, or institute has seen the need to create a code of ethics for its membership and maintain them as new challenges arise. (The American Society of Civil Engineers adopted its first code of ethics in 1912—and was still updating it in 1996.)

The codes of ethics across the engineering profession all have the same general idea, but behind the grand statements are some fairly thorny concepts. For instance, the code of ethics for the American Society of Civil Engineers has seven fundamental canons (with our notes in parenthesis):

1. Engineers shall hold paramount the safety, health, and welfare of the public in the performance of their professional duties. (This means you've done your best to make sure your building, machine, or chemical process is safe to the best of your abilities.)
2. Engineers shall perform services only in the areas of their competence. (If you're a civil engineer, don't try to do the job of a mechanical engineer.)
3. Engineers shall issue public statements only in an objective and truthful manner. (When you have people relying on your expertise, you're obligated to discuss both the positives and negatives of what you're doing—both the good it could do and the harm it could cause.)
4. Engineers shall act in professional matters for each employer or client as faithful agents or trustees, and shall avoid conflicts of interest. (In other words, if you're hired to inspect a building, don't offer to fix problems you find for a fee. This also means you accept payment only from your client and stay away from anything that looks like a bribe.)
5. Engineers shall build their professional reputation on the merit of their services and shall not compete unfairly with

others. (You need to be honest about your academic and professional accomplishments and, again, don't get involved in anything that looks like a bribe to get a contract.)

6. Engineers shall act in such a manner as to uphold and enhance the honor, integrity, and dignity of the profession. (This just means you won't intentionally do anything to harm your reputation or those of your professional colleagues.)

7. Engineers shall continue their professional development throughout their careers and shall provide opportunities for the professional development of those engineers under their supervision. (Processes are constantly changing, new materials are being introduced, and technology is charging ahead. If you are an engineer, you can plan on a lifetime of learning just to keep up with your own profession.)

Scenarios

It's hard to predict when an ethical issue could suddenly face you, or what you should do with it once you're in the middle of it. The most obvious thing for you to do as an engineer at the threshold of your career would be to take any concerns you have to your immediate supervisor.

If you're considering an engineering career, you need to know that sometimes the things you will deal with are going to be a little more complicated than just going to your boss. Mull over these fictitious scenarios and see how you'd respond according to the canons of ethics above.

(We cannot give you the absolute "right" answers. In the real world, dealing with right and wrong often includes shades of gray.)

Military Mess-Up

Let's say your company, ASAP Engineering, has a contract to build an advanced military vehicle filled with the latest battlefield electronics and weaponry. While working on the project, you notice that when the vehicle is traveling at a high rate of speed with all its electronics going full bore, the air-conditioning has a tendency to overheat from time to time. You're afraid that if personnel are forced to shut down the air-conditioning, the vehicle could overheat and lock up the electronics, thereby shutting down the entire unit—essentially turning the vehicle from a fighting machine into a battlefield sitting duck.

You talk with your superiors about your concerns, who in turn consult with the Army liaison.

The liaison points out that, first, the project is behind schedule and any major redesign of the vehicle now would add expense and delay production. The liaison and the company also note there is no data showing frequent failure of the air-conditioning system, so there is no real evidence of a major problem. The military liaison also advises there will be specialized training on the unit for the personnel who operate it and, above all else, soldiers understand there is risk to war and that no system is foolproof. Still, everyone agrees some minor adjustments might remedy the problem.

Shortly thereafter, you leave ASAP and take a job at a competing company, War Room Engineering. Three years later, you are watching the evening news and hear that three new high-tech Army vehicles suddenly shut down in the middle of combat with substantial loss of life.

According to the code of ethics previously detailed, what is your obligation? Do you contact the Army and tell them what you suspect about the vehicle? Should you contact the news media? Should you contact anyone at all, given that you no longer are with ASAP Engineering and you're not even sure what adjustments were made before it went into production?

The first canon of ethics suggests you will protect human life, but the second says you'll only issue truthful statements. You are obligated to uphold the honor of the profession, but you also are obligated to compete fairly in the marketplace.

What would you do?

Toxic Profits

You are the chief environmental engineer at a processing plant and your duties include testing and management of waste discharge into a nearby stream.

Consistently, your company has been right at, or just below, the discharge standards but you know your company could dramatically improve its record by installing another filtering apparatus before the wastewater leaves the plant. You bring up the idea, but you are turned down because of expense.

Then the company announces that it has won a new contract that will require higher production levels. You know that as production levels increase, the plant will go over the EPA discharge standard.

You advise company officials of the problem and in turn, they offer you a compromise: Accept the higher discharges for six months and risk EPA fines (and polluting the river) until the company earns enough money to install the second filter that will bring toxic waste back down to acceptable levels.

What do you do?

Underbidding

Suppose you are invited to bid on a multimillion-dollar bridge project and three rival companies also are asked to submit bids. Fortunately, your company's bid is the lowest and you get the job.

After you've begun construction, however, you notice a critical omission in your design plans that will somewhat weaken the bridge, although not enough to jeopardize public safety. Nevertheless, the omission will mean the project will not meet client specifications.

It's not too late to fix the omission but the added expense to the project would mean your company is no longer the lowest bidder. Alternatively, if your company has to eat the cost of the change, the project no longer would be profitable and quite possibly could send your company into bankruptcy, leading to a substantial loss of jobs.

The obvious question is: what should you do?

The canon of ethics would suggest that you should advise your client as soon as possible of the error and negotiate a solution. Your company supervisor, however, would likely insist that you remain quiet for the sake of all concerned.

What do you do?

In high school and college, students are taught that "right" and "wrong" are clearly marked. In the real world, those signs don't exist.

Questions of ethics and questions about what engineers knew about the projects they were working on are arising more and more often. These kinds of questions are almost certain to challenge you at some point in your career.

CHAPTER 21

What Else Can You Do?

Other places an engineering degree can take you

*"Engineers like to solve problems. If there
are no problems handily available, they will
create their own problems."*
   –Scott Adams, creator of the cartoon "Dilbert"

Here's one of your worst fears: What if you go all the way through school, right up to your senior year, and start having a nagging feeling that engineering really isn't what you want to do for the rest of your life?

Even worse, what if you've finished school, have a nice job as an engineer somewhere, and start having the same nagging feeling?

Is engineering all you've got? Can't you do anything else? Do you wonder if any other company would want you if all you could do was engineer?

Fortunately, and unfortunately, the answer is yes—even without your calculator, you are an attractive prospect.

Why People Leave

Burnout is not an unknown phenomenon in the engineering business and it comes from a variety of directions.

First and foremost, many engineers point out that it is a relentless profession where you have a difficult time leaving the office at the office. You tend to keep working on problems as you drive home at night, while you watch TV after work, and even as you lie in bed trying to fall asleep.

Much of engineering is a giant logic puzzle that professionals tend to continue working on until it's solved. The downside of that is that you never really leave work, and it's difficult to have a social life if your mind is always computing.

Another factor is education. Engineers always have to live with the challenge of keeping up-to-date on their industry and the directions it is headed. Regular attendance at conferences and symposiums are virtually mandatory. New ways of doing things are constantly being developed and if you don't keep up, you can fall behind quickly—and in the professional world, that means becoming less competitive. The pressure is heavy.

Another concern is the office environment. In other chapters we've talked about your need to work and play well with others, such as accountants, marketing departments, the legal staff, and so on. There is a certain frustration to knowing you are probably the smartest person in the meeting but may still have to "do it" someone else's way.

Don't forget about salaries either. The engineering world offers great starting salaries, but to keep your pay grade moving up, you are increasingly likely to become involved in the nontechnical side of the business. That, of course, is a good thing and a bad thing. What is certain, however, is that the higher you climb on the corporate ladder, the less actual engineering you are likely to do.

Engineering a Career Change

Fortunately for you, however, people with engineering degrees are easily able to cross into other businesses. Unfortunately, they do it all the time, leaving something of a chronic shortage in the engineering profession.

So what else does that engineering degree do for you?

"An engineering degree opens the door to many career options and allows you to do almost anything," says Leann Yoder, executive director of JETS (Junior Engineering Technical Society). "As far as a degree, it's a launch pad to other degrees. With an engineering degree, you can become a patent attorney, go to medical school, become the CEO of a Fortune 500 company. It teaches you how to problem solve."

It is not unusual for students to get engineering undergraduate degrees and immediately apply to go to law school or medical school where they are typically welcomed with open arms.

Says Keith Morris of Apex, North Carolina, "The things you learn (in engineering school) you can apply to lots of different areas and disciplines. You get a good sense in training in logic, which you can apply to anything—business, law, and so on. Law is just a bunch of logic."

In fact, it is not unusual for even advanced engineers (those who have gone all the way to getting their Professional Engineer license) to turn around and go to law school. In addition, a close look at the nation's corps of patent and trademark attorneys reveals a large percentage of engineers-turned-lawyers.

What's Going on Here?

Says Al Gray of the National Society of Professional Engineers, "Engineering is actually a very creative profession and very creative people get into it. A lot of people think engineers just sit around doing calculations, but what they're actually doing is applying science to problems and coming up with solutions. There are a lot of corporations out there that need that kind of thinking. That's why you find so many Fortune 500 companies being run by people who have engineering in their backgrounds."

To be sure, the field of engineering has contributed some of today's more widely recognized figures in non-engineering professions.

"Helping" as the Antidote for "Boring"

Cindy Wallis-Lage, an environmental health engineer for Black & Veatch based in the Kansas City area, believes the best engineers are the ones who put themselves into the project.

"Helping people—getting to know our clients, developing an understanding of their needs and providing unique solutions that address their current and future needs" is the best part of the job, she says.

"If it wasn't for the variety of projects, it would be pretty boring."

She describes her favorite project as developing the "Water Campus" in Scottsdale, Arizona. "It was a very high-tech project and it was the first of its kind," she says.

"The Water Campus is a zero-discharge facility, which means that 100 percent of the water is reused and no water is discharged to a receiving stream. This project was a milestone project within wastewater treatment because it was an innovative solution that helped ensure a sustainable water supply for that community."

Neil Armstrong, the first person to walk on the moon, was an engineering graduate of Purdue and, of course, Scott Adams, who created the heroic engineering comic character Dilbert, has an engineering background. Mystery writer and showman Alfred Hitchcock was an engineer, as is television talk show host and entertainer Montel Williams. Presidents Herbert Hoover and Jimmy Carter were both engineers.

Thomas Edison, the inventor of the light bulb, and Alexander Graham Bell, inventor of the telephone, perhaps two of the most recognized names in history, were engineers. One of the most famous CEOs of all time, Jack Welch, who built the General Electric empire, started out as an engineer. Coach Tom Landry, who built the Dallas Cowboys football team into a dynasty, also was an engineer.

On the other hand, there is the musical talent William Hung, who butchered Ricky Martin's "She Bangs" on the popular TV reality show *American Idol*. Hung was a civil engineering student at UC Berkeley when he made his famous audition for the show. Despite rejection by the judges, he has gone on to release three albums.

Says Gray, "It's not unusual these days for someone (in any walk of life) to start off in one profession and end up in another."

For instance, in a large manufacturing company you may start as an engineer, but work your way into research, and from there into product design, marketing and eventually up to management.

"An engineering degree is a great platform for a lot of different types of career," he said. "You can think and understand the technical aspects of your company, but you can also understand the creative aspects. And best of all, you're trained to solve problems."

Gray looks at his own career as a demonstration of what an engineering degree can help you accomplish. He started out life as a graduate of Rensselaer Polytechnic Institute in New York, and went into wastewater and environmental management services. Eventually he became an instructor at Penn State University in engineering and did research for the U.S. Public Health Service.

He worked in a number of engineering and management capacities for private industry and then moved into consulting. Eventually he became interested in association work, and became part of the NSPE, managing more than 40,000 members worldwide and providing a host of services to those members, almost none of which are engineering.

In other words, there really is no such thing as being "stuck" in the engineering profession.

CHAPTER 22

The Road Ahead

Some signs of where it might be going

"In the future, it's going to be more fun to be an engineer."

–Ed Richardson, Bechtel

How bright is the future of engineering, you ask? How could it be any brighter, we answer. You don't have to read this book to figure out where the future of engineering is, nor do you even have to crack open a textbook.

All you have to do is read the front page of your daily newspaper and you will find challenges that are going to need engineering solutions in the future. (All you have to do is subscribe to publications like *Popular Mechanics* to see who is working on those solutions.)

Environmental Crises

Hurricanes, fires, and earthquakes will continue and wherever they happen, there is going to be a need for emergency housing. Today, builders are researching how to replace destroyed homes in a matter of days, not months or years, with robot gantries driven by computer programs that tell the machinery where to pour concrete walls, where to leave spaces for windows and doors, where to allow for installation of utility hookups, and where to place the roofs. In theory, at least, adequate shelters could replace hundreds of shattered homes within weeks.

In places like New Orleans and elsewhere that are prone to high wind and water, engineers are realistically discussing huge barricades that could rise out of the shoreline and protect residential areas. Likewise, engineers are realistically discussing homes that are allowed to rise and float in times of sudden high water, such as in storm surges and flash floods.

Around the world, engineers are working to find ways to provide safe drinking water to people with no access to publicly treated water and to deal with the climate changes caused by global warming.

These will be some of the playgrounds of future engineers.

War Games

Likewise, clearly the future of modern warfare will rely less on human soldiers and more on technology that will give the fewest number of combatants the largest array of weapons.

The day may come when fixed-piece battles may be fought with remote-controlled tanks "commanded" hundreds of miles of away by captains with joysticks. Unmanned, silent, intelligence-gathering flying drones already survey hostile areas to pinpoint insurgents.

Everything from X-ray cameras to "sniffing" devices are being developed to find caches of weapons otherwise hidden behind walls. In the more immediate future, body armor continues to be made lighter, yet stronger, for situations that require humans to be in harm's way.

Again, engineers will solve human problems tomorrow.

The Human Touch

What will engineers do for our aging population? Can you come up with a way of monitoring the elderly without intruding on their privacy? Engineers in the United States and abroad are developing robots that will be human enough to provide companionship to older people while at the same time monitoring things like blood pressure and breathing, sending streams of data back to physicians seated at banks of computer monitors rather than in offices. Sensors may be embedded in walls someday to make homes "smart" enough to know if an occupant has fallen or simply forgotten to take his or her medication for the day.

Every day, biomedicine is grabbing headlines with new drugs that will extend the average lifespan of men and women into the 100s and, perhaps more importantly, make the quality of life for those with debilitating illnesses and crippling diseases worth living again. Synthetic biology may lead to the construction of new biological entities, including engineered bacteria to produce anti-malaria drugs.

Meanwhile, technology is racing forward to make it possible for people to communicate almost instantaneously around the world, and to find new ways to verify their identities.

Information technology, nanotechnology, and bioengineering will provide new opportunities for engineers in the years to come.

Fueling the Future

Obviously, the developed world right now runs on oil—with ever-higher prices being paid for an ever-dwindling supply—and a great deal of conflict is waged over who controls that oil. However, engineers are at the core of ameliorating those differences.

Petroleum engineers are under constant pressure to find new sources of oil and more efficient ways to bring it to the surface and get it to refineries. Nevertheless, even as those engineers do their work, other engineers are finding alternative sources of power and are developing wind, solar, geothermal, and other kinds of energy to light homes and businesses worldwide.

Not only are engineers working both sides of the petroleum issue, more engineers are finding ways for automobiles to go farther on less gas—and eventually on no gas at all.

Old Concerns and New Challenges

Even as all these promises of technology unfold, however, engineers will be confronted with a host of side issues that will either hamper or halt their progress.

What are the ethics of cloning? What are the ethics of ever-better war machines? Where is the economic balance between curing human suffering on earth and exploring the solar system? What will happen with bioengineered food?

Some problems that won't go away have engineering at their root, as well as at the center of their remedies. While some engineers work mines that take the tops off mountains to get at coal reserves and other resources, other engineers are enlisting to fight the resulting environmental damage and repair the soil with fast-growing trees and conservation practices.

In addition, there will be unimaginable new challenges. A report by the National Academy of Engineering says the "engineering profession needs to adopt a new vision for its future."

The report calls for engineers to be broadly educated, to become leaders in the public and private sectors, to be prepared to compete in the global marketplace, and to represent all segments of society. It says future engineers must be able to acquire new knowledge quickly, be adaptable and engage emerging problems, and also be prepared to communicate ideas and issues to multiple stakeholders, including government, private industry, and the public.

Every day, new ideas are being hammered and bolted into society to raise the human experience. Engineers are the ones doing that hammering and bolting.

Says Ed Richardson of Bechtel, "In the future, it's going to be more fun to be an engineer. The computers will do the rote work, so the engineers will be able to focus on the fun part—using their imagination, vision, and creativity. It's going to be more fun to be an engineer."

Rediscovering the Future

Professional Engineer J. Harrison Daniel, attached to the U.S. Department of the Interior Office of Occupational Health and Safety in Denver, says it is fascinating to watch modern engineers rediscover old ideas.

"I was part of a team 37 years ago to determine the 'best' technology for low-polluting, low-power electric power generation," he says. "We investigated concepts ranging from devices powered by wind and water to direct electric conversion concepts, such as magnetohydrodynamics.

"The range included thermo- and piezo-electric devices, liquid-vapor power condensing cycles with exotic working fluids, and even ceramic diesel engines.

"For me, the project culminated in escorting 300-watt hydrazine fuel cells to Vietnam in 1969, to be evaluated as silent battery chargers for combat troops.

"The project is my favorite as it repeatedly comes to mind as I read about the new advances in energy and power generation as if they have just been discovered."

Daniel also adds this caveat, "This project also taught me what became a consistently recurring theme through 40 years of research in the areas of energy/power generation and mining/minerals processing: If the technical community of dedicated engineers and scientists could influence energy policies without political interference, our world would be a better place."

CHAPTER 23

In Conclusion

There is no better time to be an engineer

"You have teenagers thinking they're going to make millions as NBA stars when that's not realistic for even 1 percent of them. Becoming a scientist or engineer is."
–Dean Kamen, engineer, inventor, entrepreneur, CEO

I n the end, it will be up to you to decide. Engineering could be a dream profession for you or it might not be. That's up to you.

We hope this book will make it a little easier to decide whether you should join this exciting, innovative, and fulfilling profession.

Engineering is a profession that doesn't care about your gender, your race, or your background. Even if it seems to be mostly a white man's club now, that only means there's a whole lot of room for women and minorities—and lots of organizations that want to see both in their membership.

Engineering wants you to be interested in how things work and how you can make the world a better place. You definitely need to be curious and creative.

"Engineering is about creating an idea in your head, thinking about it, and making it happen," says JETS Executive Director Leann Yoder.

You can do that.

Yes, you do need to like math and science and be competent in both subjects, but you definitely don't have to be a straight-A student in either area. As engineering student Michael Allen noted:

"Doing well in engineering is 90 percent hard work and 10 percent intelligence."

There are so many engineering disciplines and subdisciplines out there that you should be able to find one that interests you. If you're not as strong in math as you'd like to be, you can choose one where that won't be such an issue.

Obviously, education is important in this profession. You really should have at least an undergraduate degree in engineering, and education beyond that can only make you more proficient. You also have the options of pursuing engineering at the graduate level, earning certification in specific areas through your national association, and maintaining a lifelong commitment to continuing education to better yourself—not just retain your Professional Engineer's license—or all of the above.

We've tried to make sure you understand that, yes, engineering isn't the easiest course of study to follow but the rewards are definitely worth it—and we don't just mean the financial rewards of starting out at a salary one and a half to two times more than those that will be offered to your liberal arts friends. Remember the saying that engineers may sometimes have the lowest GPAs (grade point averages) on campus, but they usually have the highest salaries coming out.

Moreover, while your friends may still be searching for jobs by the time college graduation comes, you'll have been in demand for months and probably already will know where you'll be getting your first paycheck.

The global economy undoubtedly will influence your work life, and yes, computers will be there to help you along the way, as long as you see them as a tool and not a crutch.

Sure, you will face legal and ethical questions, but that can happen in most any profession. What doesn't happen in every other profession is a real, live actual opportunity to change the world in your community, your country, and maybe the entire world. As an engineer, you might just get that chance.

One thing is for sure: success in engineering—and most everything else—results from a three-point process:

1. Devise a plan.
2. Move forward.
3. Do it now.

Of the three, "do it now" is by far the most important. A good plan without action can only fail. A bad plan with enough work often succeeds. If you want to be a success, you will need to put *you* in motion.

With the way the world is moving and spinning, engineering is going to continue to be an important career and a profitable one for a great many years to come.

There is no better time to be an engineer.

Do it now.